The New Elites

GEORGE WALDEN

The New Elites

MAKING A CAREER IN THE MASSES

ALLEN LANE
THE PENGUIN PRESS

ALLEN LANE
THE PENGUIN PRESS

Published by the Penguin Group
Penguin Books Ltd, 27 Wrights Lane, London w8 5TZ, England
Penguin Putnam Inc., 375 Hudson Street, New York, New York 10014, USA
Penguin Books Australia Ltd, Ringwood, Victoria, Australia
Penguin Books Canada Ltd, 10 Alcorn Avenue, Toronto, Ontario, Canada M4V 3B2
Penguin Books India (P) Ltd, 11, Community Centre, Panchsheel Park, New Delhi – 110 017, India
Penguin Books (NZ) Ltd, Private Bag 102902, NSMC, Auckland, New Zealand
Penguin Books (South Africa) (Pty) Ltd, 5 Watkins Street, Denver Ext 4, Johannesburg 2094, South Africa

Penguin Books Ltd, Registered Offices: Harmondsworth, Middlesex, England

First published 2000
1

Copyright © George Walden, 2000
All rights reserved

The moral right of the author has been asserted

Set in 10.25/13.75 pt Linotype Sabon
Typeset by Rowland Phototypesetting Ltd, Bury St Edmunds, Suffolk
Printed and bound in Great Britain by The Bath Press, Bath

A CIP catalogue record for this book is available from the British Library

ISBN 0 713 99317 0

To my family and friends, for their patience
and – I hope – understanding.

Contents

To make a stand against the masses is, in the opinion of the majority, complete nonsense. For the masses, the numbers, the public, are themselves the powers of salvation, that association of lovers of liberty from whom salvation is to come . . . That is the result of having fought for centuries against Kings, Popes and the powerful, and having looked upon the people and the masses as something holy. It does not occur to people that historical categories change, and that now the masses are the only tyrant at the bottom of corruption.

Journals of Kierkegaard, 1834–54

Introduction

Three things this book is not. It is not another attack on political correctness, whose postulates, when they are justified, can be nagging platitudes, and whose extravagances have long since been laughed to scorn. It is not a defence of elites as currently conceived, who for all the obloquy heaped on them are mostly smart or rich enough to take care of themselves. Nor is this book a dirge about decline. Cultural lamentations can be diverting from the pen of Flaubert ('I have always tried to live in an ivory tower, but a sea of shit is beating against the walls, it's enough to bring them down') and sobering from William Morris ('That fatal division of men into the educated and degraded classes which capitalist commerce has encouraged'), but in our own day they are somehow dispiriting. The targets are unmissable, and in as much as complaints about decline are justified, they too have become platitudes. Certainly the price of a worthwhile culture is eternal vigilance, though as Marshall McLuhan observed, the price of eternal vigilance is indifference.

Moaning about mass culture seems especially pointless. However you define 'the masses', theirs is the leading chorus of the times. Yet choruses can perform well or badly. The singers are guided by conductors, martinets sometimes, with their eyes fixed on stardom and a vulgarized interpretation of the score. It is they, the populists in politics, in business, the media and the arts, who are the subject of this book. This too may appear to present an easy target, yet the problem with populism is that it is popular. Criticizing it involves asking why it is that the public tends to succumb, which involves appearing to sit in judgement on The People. To that extent this book is a critique of the workings of democracy, or ultra-democracy as I prefer to call it. It ought to be possible for democracies to stand outside themselves and take an objective look (if they don't, who will?), but in the contemporary climate raising a finger at The People will be greeted as disapprovingly as spitting in church.

The interaction between populism and its victims is rarely discussed. There is a shiftiness surrounding the subject, an atmosphere of nerviness where you can see in people's eyes that they are preparing to range themselves on the side of virtue before a word is spoken. I fancy the eyes of the God-fearing nineteenth-century *bon bourgeois* had exactly the same look when anything that fell outside the confines of what could be decently said was broached. A similar prissiness afflicts our era, though this time it is The People (whoever they might be) whose tastes and preferences are deemed beyond reproach.

The book is based on assumptions which, if not shared by the reader, will render it incomprehensible. I take it as self-evident that, providing they are open, elites are not just defensible but desirable in a democracy. My point is the difference between true and bogus, fertile and sterile elites. Genuine, democratic elites cannot be inimical to the public interest, since by definition they will be open, able and humane. Otherwise they forfeit their claim to the description. Bogus elites possess no true distinction and depend for their ascendency on money and/or membership of a particular social caste. Today they are more likely to be populist opportunists. Sometimes they contrive to be both.

My second assumption is that Britain is a country where populist elites have never been more powerful or ubiquitous. If they escape detection and criticism it is because (and this is my third assumption) our thinking about elites and the masses remains congealed in Left/Right configurations, a kind of arrested development that remains widespread in our culture.

Only by abstracting oneself from these decayed conventions is it possible to see what is happening, not in two-dimensional caricature, but in the round.

Three key terms – democracy, the elites and the masses – seem to me in need of redefinition. In this book each will be used in what some may feel to be the opposite of its normal sense. That is because of my belief that populist democracies are undemocratic, and that the elites and the masses have ceased to be the people we thought they were. To some, my vision of society may appear upside down. Naturally I would suggest that it is they who, by failing to adjust their perceptions as reality reshapes itself around them, find themselves standing on their heads.

For all its vaunted liberties, Britain remains a country of cliques and convention: we are free to say what we like, but if anyone is to listen what we say must fall within the confines of the game. What will not be tolerated is criticism of the game itself, or suggestions that there may be other, more interesting games to be played. One response to this soft totalitarianism of opinion is silence: as Wittgenstein almost said, whereof one cannot speak rationally and be understood it is better not to speak at all. Another is to argue one's case regardless, which is what this book attempts to do.

Its departures from accepted norms of democratic ingratiation will of course be condemned as elitist in themselves. In our antiquated up/down, Left/Right thinking, so it goes. All I can say is that, if you can't please everyone, all the more reason to describe things as you see them, even if it pleases no one. There is at least one accusation I shall be spared: a book whose intention is to expose the depredations of populism cannot be accused of angling for popularity.

I

In Search of the Elites

The future belongs to crowds.

Don DeLillo

'Elitism', the woman rapped out over dinner, 'is a bad word.'

'Absolutely,' echoed her partner. They were an echoing couple.

A moment before the woman had been affable, relaxed; now she seemed seized by fervour. The natural thing would have been to deflect the conversation with some light remark, but in the wake of her malediction light remarks – easily mistaken for elitist irony – were out of order. There was an instant's silence. It was as if grace had been said and the company felt it should cross itself and murmur 'The Lord protect us' before falling back to its food.

The woman's pronunciamento seemed at variance with her persona. She was expensively dressed, self-assured, a figure of authority. Her partner exuded the same confident worldliness. Also, the observation seemed in conflict with her surroundings: the dinner was in an exclusive club, where the two of them seemed at ease. When someone spoke it was to ask what elite meant today. The woman fell to thinking. How would I define it myself, I reflected, and came up with a blank. I waited for someone to quote Matthew Arnold – 'the best that is known and thought in the world' – determined that on no account would it be me. It was an inadequate definition at the best of

times, and this was the worst. I could imagine the come-back
all too easily:

'*Best*? It depends what you mean.'

'Well, something that's better than anything else.'

'Who's to say?'

'Well, someone has to say . . .'

'You mean some people are intrinsically superior to others?'

'That's not what I said . . .'

Later (it is always later) I remembered a passage in Saul
Bellow's novella *The Bellarosa Connection*:

As for Sorella, she was a woman with great powers of intelligence, and
in these democratic times, whether you are conscious of it or not, you
are continually in quest of higher types. I don't have to draw you maps
and pictures. Everyone knows what standard products and interchangeable parts signify, understands the operation of the glaciers
on the social landscape, planing off the hills, scrubbing away the
irregularities. I'm not going to be tedious about this.

Higher types? Lucky I hadn't remembered.

The exclusive club served superb wines. The company was in
relaxed mood, and showed no enthusiasm for a row. No one
offering a definition of elitism, or presuming to defend the
indefensible, the conversation moved on in that hurried, self-
conscious way it does when subjects of such troubling topicality
arise that people will do anything rather than follow them up.
The British react to the subject of elitism as their Victorian
ancestors did to sex; it troubles them deeply for reasons they
would prefer not to think about, their consciences are not quite
as clean as they would like, so they opt for a prudish reserve.
For me our collective silence had settled the point. That brief,
edgy exchange had confirmed three things in my mind: that
elitism is at the centre of our social and cultural debate, that all
righteous people are against it – and that no one can say with
any certainty exactly what it is.

This seems something of an omission since, whatever it is, a movement seems underway to extirpate it from society. The Government condemns it, the BBC are fervently against it, the media despise it, writers and artists go to great lengths to disclaim it, the schools inoculate children against it as they once did smallpox or diphtheria. Yet few stop to ask what the idea means in twenty-first-century Britain. In mass democracies, where the offence of elitism is concerned, condemnation and sentencing take precedence over definition, let alone proof.

Politicians have long since learned to watch their language. 'I look forward to a world that will not only be safe for democracy and diversity,' said President Kennedy thirty-two years ago, 'but also for distinction.' Presidential speech-writers would erase that last phrase today. The sentence would stop at 'diversity', with its mellifluous vagueness and suggestion of the horizontal rather than the vertical. Which would be undemocratic, since it is hard to see ordinary folk taking offence at the idea that a little distinction was a desirable aim for all. The whole point of America is that anyone can become its distinguished President.

The opposite of elitism is currently inclusiveness. Applied to the need to embrace within society the economic or cultural underclass, or to guard against racism, there seems little amiss with the term. What is misleading is to see elites and inclusiveness as incompatible. In a true democracy a member of what we now call the underclass would have a fair chance of gravitating upwards to join society's elites: to become a rich businessman or woman, a distinguished writer or scientist, a leading politician. Yet that is not the current thinking. As so often, we appear to be more concerned with looking down in compassion than with enabling the objects of our pity to look up in hope.

Such is the feeling against elites that one could almost imagine a movement to ban the term from polite conversation; if words like 'nigger' or 'queer' are seen as offensive to minorities, 'elite' is surely more heinous still – an offence to entire societies. Yet a ban would be problematical: we would find ourselves up against what our dictionaries term ordinary usage. In some contexts the word continues to be employed in the same benign, common-sensical way it was two hundred years ago: to designate things of particular excellence. For example, it remains acceptable to send elite troops into battle (where would journalists be without the phrase?) in defence of democracy. Elite footballers can also figure in democracy's favorite sport, whose players are bought and sold and segregated into leagues according to their scores in a way many schools remain reluctant to do, and whose star performers are at liberty to spend their millions on products of particular excellence, such as BMWs or celebrity blondes.

Similarly we have no problem with elite brain surgeons, assuming they are not reserved for elitist brains, or with the arcane hierarchies of medicine (Mr and Mrs for surgeon). Just as we prefer the best marksmen to defend us, so we depend on the best doctors we can get to keep us alive. The more elite our personal medicine men are, and the clearer their competences are designated by rank and degree, the better we like it. In a materialist age, that too is natural: having no immortal souls to consign to God we become all the more choosy when it comes to deciding to whom we consign our mortal bodies. Serving a practical and popular function as they do, doctors are exempt from anti-elitist strictures. Abolishing their system of ranking, or paying them the same, would make excellent egalitarian sense, but then the most equal of our instincts is our unwillingness to die. The same is true of science in general. Scientists have something of an elitist image – their Nobel Prizes, their esoteric language, their almost mystical powers and occasional cold arrogance. Yet they are perceived as doing practical things, and that is what gives them such popularity as they enjoy.

Film stars, sportsmen and other mass entertainers are another exempt category. Though at the very pinnacle of society, these are people who serve the practical function of supplying democracy with the much-needed circuses to go with the now abundant bread, and whose popularity entitles them to see themselves, and to be seen by others, as 'higher types'. What invite dis-approval are power elites, intellectual elites, elite writers (unless their subjects are horse-racing or crime), or anything smacking of an 'elitist' culture. All are perceived as arbitrary or exclusive, an affront to the common man.

Social elites are equally suspect – unless the socialites fall into the category of celebrities, in which case their mass appeal excuses their conspicuous spending, their cliquishness and aristocratic affectations of being above convention or, when it comes to narcotics, above the law. All this is, in its way, natural. Unlike the stars and celebrities, the upper classes have few fans; those whose most heartfelt desire is to join their number tend to keep quiet about it.

The fine distinctions, the inclusions and exemptions, prolifer-ate endlessly. It is a strange creature, our notion of elitism, a bird of ever-changing hues and wings of variable geometry. For some it is a carrion crow, to be shot out of the sky on sight. For others it is a glittering creature at whom they gaze aloft to marvel at its flight. The distinction between good forms of elitism and bad can be dismissed as hypocrisy, yet behind the seeming arbitrariness there is a logic of sorts. Two things would seem to divide acceptable from unacceptable elitism: utilitarian-ism and mass appeal. An idealist might prefer William Morris's formula – usefulness and beauty – but that lacks the magic ingredient: inclusiveness. We live when we do, and the useful and the popular are concepts that most succinctly define the spirit of the age. Conversely, whatever serves no practical func-tion and is not open to the many to understand and enjoy with minimal effort is dismissed as elitist in the most reprehensible sense.

Yet things are not so simple. Even this apparently clear-cut distinction breaks down when exposed to daily practice. Like all moral (or moralistic) codes, anti-elitism has its intricacies, its grey areas, its mystifications and perversities to perplex the uninitiated. The monarchy, one would have thought, would fall foul of the anti-elites, yet somehow it is reprieved from the mental guillotine. Royal persons may not appear to serve much in the way of a practical purpose, yet the media have found a use for them, and popular they most certainly are. The public know what they like, they like royalty, and were infatuated with Princess Diana. This time it is not a case of the masses showing themselves to be more broad-minded than their spokesmen, since the monarchy continues to get an understanding press, even on the Left, which has always had trouble with the maddening inconsistencies of the people.

What the public appear to be telling us about the monarchy is on any enlightened view retrograde, sexist and undemocratic: that you are a superior person if you are born into the Royal Family, and especially superior if you are a young woman who chances to be good-looking and who marries into it. Should you be a commoner and a male of indifferent looks and, by dint of talent and application, make yourself an expert on classical Greek literature, then you are suspected of elitism and placed, mentally, under armed guard. The conclusion would seem to be clear. In our populist democracy it is all right to be royal, sexy and not over-bright, not all right to be plain, a commoner and smart. Which makes nonsense of democracy. But there you are: the people, being sovereign, must be allowed their little quirks and contradictions. A wise man would do well not to argue the point publicly, since in mass societies attempts at rational argument, as Schumpeter observed, can bring out the animal spirits.

A further example of confusion in the anti-elitist camp: whereas the populist code must surely be international, concerned as it is for the brotherhood of the common man, its application varies, for no good reason, from country to country. A glance at opera and ballet makes the point. As forms of art which enjoy limited appeal, both offend against the anti-elitist spirit; unless, that is, you happen to be an Italian, in the case of opera, or a Russian balletomane. Somewhere across the time zones opera and ballet cease to be elitist and become popular forms of art. Whether this is because Anglo-Saxons are backward in their artistic education, or because the Italians and Russians are backward in their social understanding, no one can say.

Nowhere are the contradictions more evident than in education. Opening what are seen as recondite areas of study or taste to the appreciation of the many, for example by ensuring that a grounding in classics is more widely available, cuts no ice with the populist. The very study of the classics, unless carried out in a carefully sanitized manner (daily lives of the Romans) and in our own demotic (did not the Romans speak demotic too?), carries a taint. Again a strange logic is at work, as we reach the position where there is only one thing more reprehensible than having elite tastes, and that is trying to spread them, so as to make them less elite. If intellectual elites are seen as exclusive it surely follows that the more they open themselves to all comers, the better. Otherwise anti-elitism risks becoming a recipe for the propagation of ignorance amongst the many, whose result would be to heighten divisions between the mass and the lucky few. Though even that has its rationale, since in a perverse way conflict between the few and the many is exactly what the more doctrinaire anti-elitist seems anxious to promote.

The doctrine would be easier to understand if it were clear that it reflected the public mood. Then the only response would be to count their legions compared to your own and, executing a low deferential bow, scuttle to your hole. But when it comes to elitism and elites, public opinion – as we have seen in the case of royalty – is ambiguous. Often it is not 'the masses' (a term whose definition we shall come to) who impose these arbitrary codes and distinctions: it is middle-class, liberal-minded folk purporting to speak on their behalf. The most striking aspect of anti-elitism as a social and cultural doctrine in Britain is that it is propagated not from below, but largely from above.

British football fans took Eric Cantona to their hearts despite his being French, which was bad enough, but in disregard of his weakness for philosophizing – a well-known predilection of the French elitist type: 'I have never, and will never, find any difference between the pass from Pelé to Carlos Alberto in the Final of the World Cup in 1970 and the poetry of the young Rimbaud.' Not every fan is likely to have understood what the Frenchman was on about, yet far from resenting their hero talking over their heads, or bristling at his pretension, as according to their middle-class mentors they should, they appear not to have minded. Perhaps they were secretly impressed that their hero could kick imposing-sounding names like Rimbaud around as deftly as the ball?

There are times when it becomes hard to take prevailing attitudes to elites and elitism seriously, moments when the discussion becomes a lowering experience in itself, a pointless argument that quickly dissolves into incoherence or hypocrisy, and is best left to zealots. The subject descends too easily into a social game. When it comes to identifying who is guilty of elitism and who is not, you ease back into your prejudices and take your choice. A list of society's offenders would be as long as it would be capricious. In Britain it would include:

Monarchists of all social classes (over two-thirds of the population, according to polls).

All those who send their children to private schools (7 per cent), or would do so if they had the money (over 50 per cent, according to the Independent Schools Information Service).

All opera buffs, Schubert lovers, Wagner fanatics and listeners to atonal music (figure unknown).

Anyone who has ever experienced a murderous spasm when hearing pop music played at full volume in public places, or by builders working on their houses.

Anyone who has ever voted, or contemplated voting, Conservative.

Anyone who has ever voted Labour, knowing the candidate to have been privately educated, a monarchist or an occasional listener to opera, Schubert or atonal music.

Anyone who describes themselves, or has been described, as upper class.

Anyone who is middle class but aspires to be upper class.

Anyone who is lower class but aspires to be middle class, in the hope that their children might one day take the final step in the progression.

Anyone who prefers the past to the present in any respect.

People with large amounts of money, and those who would kill to have it.

Anyone who employs, or would like to employ, a domestic servant.

Domestic servants whose regard for their employers is based to any degree on their status or their wealth, i.e. on their ability to employ them.

People with racist or sexist inclinations. This includes anyone who claims that men are superior to women, or vice versa, or that any race or nationality is superior to any other in any respect – this being tantamount to saying that some races or nationalities are inferior to others in some respects.

Geneticists who are coming to believe that personal attributes, including positive attributes, are more likely to be inherited than acquired.

Scientists, especially geneticists, who show signs of getting above themselves, convinced they can explain the world.

Subscribers to *Country Life* magazine and all visitors to Ascot, with or without hats.

People who hunt pretty much anything except fish.

Anyone on horseback except cowboys, policemen and the late Princess Diana.

Anyone in Rolls Royces except pop stars, fashion gurus, footballers, restaurateurs and the late Princess.

People who prefer holidaying in France, Thailand or the

Caribbean – anywhere except England – with due exception for certain parts of Spain, which have been converted into an England with sun.

Those afflicted by elitist attitudes or aspirations seem a mighty large group. To their number must be added inverts of elitism, which comes to much the same thing, and who include:

People who insist that they enjoy English beaches far more than those of the Caribbean, Thailand, etc.

Anyone who claims to be driven mad by royal rubbish in the media but who reads or watches the stuff just the same.

Anyone who claims that South African/Australian/Chilean/Bulgarian/American wines are self-evidently equal or superior to the French product.

Upper- or middle-class people who affect an Estuary accent.

Anyone who dresses down for social reasons.

Parents who ache to dress down, but are afraid of inviting the scorn of their children, who have already dressed down and changed their accents to avoid sounding and appearing like their parents.

Parents who claim to adore their childrens' music but who can never be found listening to it privately and for pleasure.

People who were educated at private schools who say they were hell and undemocratic, then send their children to similar institutions, on the grounds that they are day schools, so that is all right.

People who say they have heard there is a marvellous comprehensive somewhere in the vicinity.

Parents who say that examinations are not everything, what matters is that children should be happy, while forcing their own to work their backsides off to do well in examinations.

Fishermen against bloodsports.

People who say they would be only too willing to pay more taxes, providing they can be sure the money would go to the poor, while availing themselves of every tax break they can, legitimately or otherwise.

People who claim that all creativity, cultural life and honesty in human relations begin north of Watford.

Upper-and middle-class people who take their children to McDonalds, do not finish their meal, declare it to be wonderful, and never go there again.

Expensively educated people who make a show of cultural tolerance, when in fact they enjoy mass-market books or TV programmes because, for all their education, they are lazy-minded or not too bright.

Yet a third category (we are fecund in social deceit) needs to be added. This consists of self-styled social or intellectual elites whose superiority is apparent to no one but themselves – a category so numerous as to prohibit examples on grounds of space. Putting all three groups together – the overt, the covert and the would-be elitists – we get something approaching the totality of the population. Many of their attitudes are indeed reprehensible; in that sense anti-elitists are right to chastise them and to seek out and expose their presumptions or double standards. On the other hand, eliminating reprehensible attitudes, like Chairman Mao's campaign to eliminate sparrows, would be an impossible task, there being just too many of them. Also because sparrows, like other high fliers, can be useful creatures, on whom entire ecologies can turn out to depend. By exterminating hundreds of millions of them the Chairman left the field clear for the pests on whom they fed. The result was the death by starvation of millions of humans, along with the sparrows. There is surely a moral here.

Anti-elitism in its modern guise dates back to the sixties. In so far as the term denoted a thawing of frozen hierarchies, a freeing of thought, the liberation of women and the breaking down of repressive sexual codes, it was a welcome movement. For all its excesses, few would seriously propose a return to the *status quo ante*. But that was over a third of a century ago. Since that time the sixties revolt has taken the path of all revolutions: it has grown old and fixed in its ways. Then it was youthful, anti-authoritarian – a joyous rebellion. Now its spiritual descendants have become narrow-minded, intolerant authoritarians themselves in their pursuit of populist dogma.

The circle has turned and a new conformism is in danger of replacing the old. It is not for nothing that the generation raised in the sixties and who now find themselves in positions of power are frequently characterized by reflexes of control. As the dictates of populism take over from 'elite' values people have begun to glance mentally over their shoulders before taking a step aside from the crowd, or appearing to suggest that there may be something higher or more enduring than the mood of the moment. The rooting out of what are seen as elitist attitudes or assumptions, in culture especially, has become the grim sport of democracy – or rather of those acting in democracy's name.

It is not as if the gains of the sixties revolution were threatened. If we leave aside the petty snobberies listed above, the risk of contamination by thoroughgoing elitist ideologies in the life of the man or woman in the street would seem on a par with that of contracting Creutzfeldt-Jakob disease by eating beef on the bone. The sensibilities of clean-living democrats are unlikely to be affronted by too many examples of elitism in their daily round. Consider the average twenty-four hours in the life of the average family.

The morning papers are unlikely to aim too far over its head. The headlines and blurbs our average family glances at over breakfast will be 'exclusive' in name but not in nature. In tabloid or in broadsheet, the values of entertainment and distraction increasingly dominate those of analysis or information. The fare deemed fit for general consumption, regardless of class or income, differs more in presentation than in essence: sex and models, model sex, ministerial scandals, a 'human' story or two, celebrity disclosures, a posthumous episode in the Charles/ Diana soap. As for the 'lifestyle choice' features that have replaced more forbidding fare, the most striking thing about them is that there is no choice whatsoever. Shorn of fake sophistication, the recommended style of life for all ages, classes and conditions is fundamentally the same: slim, sex-crazed and rigorously uncerebral.

As the day has begun, so it will continue. The children of both tabloid- and broadsheet-reading parents will go to primary schools where (aside from the small cohort of prep school children) the very tables at which they sit will be arranged in artfully dishevelled fashion so as to avoid any impression of an arbitrary hierarchy between the teacher and the taught. A similar prudence will characterize the morning assembly, should one take place. If the Almighty is alluded to it will not be as a supreme power threatening retribution from above, but as a good democratic guy. As for the lessons, they will be meticulously pitched to suit average abilities.

Meanwhile, their parents will spend the day in open-plan offices and work teams designed to improve efficiency by stressing collective endeavour, rather than by a top–down managerial approach. Later they will return home, where adults and children will watch most of their statutory 3.61 hours of television or video. By this stage of the day the chances of contagion by elitist notions are at their lowest; the ban on programmes that could be described as highbrow does not end with the nine o'clock rule, unlike those with a semi-pornographic content.

I am not condemning all modern teaching methods or new ways of treating employees, or disputing the entertainment function of TV and the press. The point is simply that the average citizen is not exactly in thrall to out-moded canons of taste and behaviour handed down from above.

Traditional elites have not vanished. Hierarchies are resilient and an upper caste in the old sense continues to exist. Of course there are powerful cliques, obviously there is back-scratching, nepotism and the rest: old Etonians who cry 'victimization' should one of them be jailed, the Oxbridge set, a rump House of Lords, the higher civil servants, the spouters of Latin tags (rare now, except in our imaginations), judges who don't know their Snoop Doggy Dogg from their Dylan, the silly hats over sillier faces at Ascot. But it beggars credulity to be told that such are the people who currently order society or impose its values. Taken together, the cultural influence they exercise is less than that of an education authority in the Midlands, or of a TV show commanding an audience of 15 million.

It is enough to attempt to mouth the words 'the governing classes' to see how things have changed. Not so long ago, it meant something. Now the words have all but lost their significance. It is by no means certain who the upper classes are, and if they have ceased to govern in the accepted sense it is lucky for them since government is neither as rewarding, interesting nor as prestigious as it was. In these pragmatic times what matters in deciding who is top dog is commercial power and cultural influence in the broadest sense, and there is a world of difference between a self-styled superior caste and the real movers and shakers of society.

Once the (real or affected) values of the allegedly upper classes cease to reverberate through every social level, or to be brandished as a model, hierarchies are dislodged and pyramids flattened. Except in its own imagination, what used to be known as high society ceases to form an elite in the modern sense; it shrivels to the status of a social caste or economic interest group. If such people are the main threat to democracy then democrats can sleep peacefully in their beds.

The truth is that the anti-elitist's fox has long been shot. If not dead, it is certainly crippled, and in no position to impose its will. Yet the heresy hunt goes on. The less visible the traditional elites and the less evident their influence, the more insistent the campaign against them and their supposed values. In this way mass democracies can find themselves veering towards authoritarian attitudes, as populism becomes the only acceptable approach to political, social or cultural life. In the calls for vigilance against elitist thinking there are faint echoes of regimes where the revolution is never safe till every enemy, real or imaginary, has been liquidated.

The atmosphere of apprehension that can result reaches into the most unlikely places. In a recent edition of the BBC's *Gardeners' Question Time* a champion rose-grower volunteered an apology for his passion. Speaking in a quavering voice suffused with guilt, the expert on roses said that he knew it was wrong to admire them as much as he did, but seeing them dancing in the breeze he could not help thinking of them as ballerinas. He knew this was elitist of him (his word), but he had admired the beauty of roses all his life and, elitist as it was (he kept repeating the term, in a sort of remorseful incantation), he found it hard to change now.

The response of the average listener would lie somewhere between laughter and sympathy. For all his absurd fears, with his acute sense of smell the rose-grower had caught a whiff of something in the air. He was afraid of appearing a rose-snob. His only defence – that he bred them because he admired beauty for its own sake, and thought of them as ballerinas – got him into another corner. Breeding, beauty, ballerinas? Had he been a Nazi scientist expressing remorse for engaging in experiments in eugenics the poor old man could scarcely have sounded more contrite.

It is a strange society which raises the anti-elitist banner ever higher at the very moment when mass tastes, as absolute as the whims of monarchs, are insinuating themselves into every crevice of our lives. Thirty-five years ago anti-elitism was a liberating force. Now it is constraining, a secular religion with its dogmas, its clerisy, its cloudy hermeneutics. It is hard to see how populism can find new territory to conquer, yet somehow it does, and the pressures to conform are endless and uncompromising. The sixties revolution has more than done its work. Still the glacier Bellow spoke of creeps over the social landscape, planing off the hills, scrubbing away the irregularities.

Aside from the sixties, the last time elites were the focus of debate was at the beginning of the century. It was the era of democratic ferment in Europe – trade unionism, the growth of socialism, revolutionary stirrings – and the reaction produced the classic defence of elites. The theorists involved would today be seen as having been 'on the wrong side of history', but that is no reason to disregard them. The phrase only makes sense in a Panglossian world where everything turns out for the best: the Mensheviks were on the wrong side of history, they just happened, in opposing revolutionary violence, to be right. So it is worth glancing back to see what these outcasts of history said, not in a mood of nostalgia or of retrospective judgementalism but as objectively as possible, which means taking account of the conditions of the times.

The main apologists for elites, the so-called classical elitists, were an influential trio: Vilfredo Pareto, Robert Michels and Gaetano Mosca. It is unfortunate that two of the three were Italian, in that the Italian for elite is *aristocrazia*. Also, the names have a mafiosi ring. The fact that they have been dubbed the 'Machiavellians', since they appeared to share the Florentine's belief that the minority must inevitably rule the majority, does nothing to predispose us in their favour. Still less are we impressed to learn that the Nazis borrowed aspects of their thinking for their perverted purposes.

Yet the most casual acquaintance with their work reveals that Pareto, Michels and Mosca were neither supporters of defunct aristocracies, cynics nor fascists. Certainly they were concerned about the advent of the mass society, but that was and remains a permissible stance. Now that we have one, it is worth seeing how far their apprehensions were justified. Frequently they asked the right questions or made a persuasive diagnosis, only to come up with dubious answers; not exactly a new phenomenon where writers and intellectuals are concerned. Marx did much the same.

Today personalities influence us as much as ideas, and on paper the CVs of the Machiavellians do not look good. Pareto (1848–1923), a gifted man and a pioneer of econometrics, fits our conventional notion of an elitist (bad sense) most closely. He came from a noble family, was proud and mordant, and had disrespectful things to say about the masses (though he was hardly more disdainful than Lenin, who described them as 'slumbering, inert, hidebound and dormant'). Today Pareto would be seen as an entertaining critic of modish thinking, with his ironic style and distrust of fads. Ironically, he himself was to become something of a fad in America when his works were translated in the thirties; the rise of Hitler and the Second World War put paid to that.

To get the flavour of the man, here he is in a throwaway passage criticizing teetotalism in his book of 1923, *The Rise and Fall of Elites: An Application of Theoretical Sociology*. Noting that abstinence had no effect on the people but was an influence on the leisured classes, he wrote:

All this asceticism of the higher classes will result solely in making them a little more anaemic, a little more abject, a little less able to defend themselves. What do you expect from people who eat no meat, drink no wine, and modestly lower their eyes when they see a beautiful woman? They may go and become monks in the Thebaid, but they cannot fight and win the battle of life.

Pareto's belief in the desirability of elites was more nuanced and rational than this squib suggests. He believed in the inequality of individual endowment (no great surprise to modern geneticists), and that society was divided into a lower and upper stratum. This in turn was subdivided into a governing and non-governing elite. To us this appears simplistic, not to say reactionary. But Pareto did not see the governing classes as belonging to a single social group and his elites were not hereditary. He favoured upward mobility, and though far from being an instinctive democrat he believed that democratic elites were least dangerous for individual liberty. Change in the ruling class was necessary to avoid stagnation, and in any event history showed that the disappearance of one elite and its replacement by another was inevitable, as more vigorous and able people took over from defunct *aristocrazias*, including talent from lower down society. That is what he meant by his famous saying 'history is a graveyard of aristocracies'. Elites, in other words, come and go.

His definition of the leaders of society was broad-minded, anticipating both open elites and the celebrity culture. For him an attractive society vamp was as much a member of the elite as the successful businessman or politician, in the sense that, like it or not, she was good at her trade. More contentious were his preference for charismatic leaders, his suspicions of social progress, his view that excessive humanitarianism rotted the will of the governing classes to govern and his conviction that the minority must inevitably hold sway over the majority by either force or guile – the lion and the fox of the Machiavellian tradition. When Pareto died the pro-Mussolini press regretted that he had not been a fascist, but did him the 'honour' of claiming that he had influenced fascist thought. Raymond Aron, the French political scientist, is a more reputable source. For him Pareto was ultimately a liberal.

Robert Michels (1876–1936) was a German sociologist who began his political involvement as a social-democrat. For a long time this debarred him from a professorial chair in Germany. In the twenties he praised Mussolini for being a charismatic leader, and got a chair in Italy. Yet Michels is no easier to pigeonhole than Pareto. He came to his belief in the inevitability of elites from a background in left-wing organizations, and was one of the first to bring psychology and sociology to the study of politics. His most famous work, *Political Parties: A Sociological Study of the Oligarchical Tendencies of Modern Democracy*, was published in 1911. Its lugubrious title notwithstanding, this is no tediously theoretical tome, and the lessons he drew from his experience were highly practical. He noticed how few genuine workers attended trade union meetings, how the leaders of the Left were almost invariably educated men and women from the middle or upper classes, and that it was their will and interests, rather than those of the working class, that tended to prevail.

'In theory, the principal aim of socialist and democratic parties is the struggle against oligarchy in all its forms. The question therefore arises how we are to explain the development in such parties of the very tendencies against which they have declared war.' An excellent question, still pertinent in British Labour or American Democratic politics today. For our purposes the crucial part of his argument was his contention that the emergence of elites, even in democratic parties and movements, was not something temporary that would disappear as the lower classes became better educated. Elites were a primary fact of any complex system of human organization, and it was from the most ambitious form of social organization of his times – the socialist movement – that Michels drew his 'iron law of oligarchies'. What he meant was that in any organization hierarchies of one kind or another are bound to emerge. Not necessarily benevolent ones either, but people who would invariably replace existing elites with their own.

Recent historical experience has converted this insight into a truism. A glance at the rise of the *nomenklatura* of communist countries, the behaviour of many a trade union leader in the West, at the cliques and clans of President Clinton's White House, or for that matter at the spoils system and patronage in the British Labour Party elected in 1997 ('after victory,' wrote Pareto, 'new elites become more rigid and more exclusive') makes Michels's theory less pessimistic and more realistic by the year.

Mosca (1858–1941) was a founder of the discipline of political science. A jurist, constitutionalist, politician and senator, he too believed that societies are invariably ruled by elites, be they military, ecclesiastical or aristocracies of wealth or merit. Mosca was more friendly towards modern democracy than the sceptical Pareto. His main contribution was to refine the notion of the circulation of elites. He was in favour of meritocrats, though not of a meritocracy: namely, he believed that society should not be run entirely according to merit, but by a broader elite. The more one reads of him the harder it becomes to slot him into our standard categories and dismiss him out of hand as a classical conservative. Indeed, there is a striking convergence between his thinking on elites and that of Antonio Gramsci (1891–1937), an idol of the Left.

The hardening of Left/Right divisions in twentieth-century politics and the reluctance of both traditions to re-examine fundamentals has tended to obscure the truth: that Mosca, the alleged reactionary, and Gramsci, the alleged revolutionary, were at bottom both democratic elitists. These are no fusty, theoretical disputes, and two conclusions are central to our times. The first is that an 'elitist' is not necessarily an anti-democrat, then or now. The second is that, then and increasingly now, Left/Right modes of thought are of limited relevance to the debate.

Seen from today's vantage point, and with an indulgent eye, the Machiavellians could best be described as democratic pessimists – a broad and not dishonourable church that could be extended to include anyone from Gramsci (with his 'pessimism of the intellect, optimism of the will') to de Gaulle and Winston Churchill (democracy is the least bad system of government) or to E. M. Forster for his 'Two Cheers for Democracy'. The reason we hear so little about the Machiavellians today is not simply that their era of wars and revolutions was so radically different from our own as to leave them with little to say to us. Largely it is because, like the great Florentine himself, they are an ideological inconvenience. Many of their analyses, difficult for our generation to swallow, are also hard to refute in the light of experience since their time. To ignore their work on the grounds that some of their attitudes were distasteful would be like declining to take Bertrand Russell seriously as a philosopher because in the postwar years he advocated using nuclear weapons against Russia while America had a monopoly (later he switched to nuclear disarmament), or to refuse to read a line of the novels of Graham Greene because he once announced to a rightly incredulous world that he would prefer to live in Soviet Russia rather than America.

The Machiavellians were by no means ignored in their time: their theories influenced Weber and Schumpeter as well as Gramsci. The main difference was that, whereas the two Germans stressed the need for a political elite produced by a competition for votes, the Machiavellians emphasized the gulf between strong, charismatic leaders and the led. What is important today is to separate the perennial from the time-bound aspects of their thinking. The fact is that, in the so-called century of the masses, in no country – capitalist, socialist, social-democratic, communist or fascist – have elites disappeared. In mild or severe form, whether it be the Nazi dictatorship, the Soviet Politburo, the TUC in its heyday or the military-industrial complex, the twin dictums of the 'iron law of oligarchy' and that 'history is a graveyard of aristocracies' appear to have prevailed.

Pessimists they may have been, but when pessimists turn out to have been right, it is time to take note. The question is not whether elites should exist. If the Machiavellians were right they will exist in any society, however democratic. What matters is who they are today.

In the postwar period the most convincing analysis of elites came not from the Right but from the liberal Left: C. Wright Mills's book *The Power Elite*. Though a professor of sociology, Mills was less concerned with theory than with the reality he saw before him, and it is a scintillating work. It aimed to expose those who exercised, in Mills's view undemocratically, sway over people's lives, and he had no doubts who they were: 'As decisions tend to become total in their consequence the leading men in each of the three domains of power – the warlords, the corporation chieftains, the political directorate – tend to come together, to form the power elite of America.'

His analysis enjoyed a wide success, not least because it had echoes in Europe. Like Pareto, Michels and Mosca, he was reacting against the tendencies of the time. His book appeared in 1956, one of the key dates in the Cold War, which scarred the twentieth-century consciousness so deeply that we have yet to assimilate fully the fact that it is over. Machiavelli believed that one of the justifications for minority rule was the demands of foreign and defence policy, of which the populace knew little, and a side-effect of the Cold War was to keep the idea of the necessity of elites alive, notwithstanding the sixties.

The Cold War appeared to validate the need for powerful leaders, whether Churchill to warn against the Iron Curtain or John F. Kennedy to face down the Russians in the Cuba crisis. (Both of them, as it happened, were in their different ways products of aristocratic families.) Secrecy, the quasi-military mentality of hierarchies, the need for the subordination of nations and individuals to the wider scheme of things and the demands of production – all these were congenial to the theory of elites. For Mills the main power elite of his time was the military-industrial complex. Hence his talk of 'warlords' and 'chieftains'. Innovative and important as his book was, especially in showing how new elites form in response to circumstances, a large chunk of Mills's analysis went down with the Berlin Wall.

There seems little need to emphasize how times have changed. Talk of foreign policy or military elites has little resonance outside the professional circles whose habit it is to define themselves in this way. Fashion elites and style gurus are today more likely to command public interest and respect. Remnants of the military-industrial complex still exist, not least in countries prominent in the export of weapons, such as America, France and Britain, and their influence still needs to be fingered and called to account. But by weakening the importance of foreign and defence policy, the end of the global struggle with communism punctured the heart of the 'power elite'. Neither the 'warlords' nor the 'political directorate' are what they were. Nor can the moral (or moralistic) imperative of the Cold War any longer be used (or misused, as it was by McCarthy) to increase social control. All that is left intact of Mills's triumvirate of power are the 'corporation chieftains' who, far from waning, have gone global. It would be a mistake to underestimate their power, but one leg is not enough on which to stand an analysis of modern elites.

The debates about elites earlier in the century were provoked by the rise of the mass society and of the Marxist Left. The passing of communism, the failures of democratic socialism and the triumph of neo-liberal economics have comprehensively scrambled the old arguments about the elites and the masses. Mills's view that his ruling castes were not a conspiracy, but were made up of people who came together socially and functionally to achieve their goals, was compatible with Mosca's theory. For all America's egalitarianism, there too power elites had emerged. But their composition changes and, perceptive as it was (its chapter on the culture of celebrity reads well today), Mills's analysis of who the elites were in his time is of limited value at the turn of the millennium. History can be a graveyard of sociologists, as well as aristocracies, and the ideas in Mills's study need to be readapted, and in some cases stood on their heads to suit the times.

The next idea which came along in the sporadic debate about elites is now almost equally dated. This was the optimistic notion that the 'ruling class' was in reality increasingly composed of professional or technical groups (a point alluded to by Mills), whose interests occasionally coincided but whose threat to society was limited by checks and balances, and by the fact that they were largely open. These were the post-1960s, and the hope was that the circulation of elites would be based more on ability and less on class. This benign prospect conjured the image of a series of formerly exclusive golf clubs to which promising players could henceforth be admitted, their subscriptions to be paid or subsidized by the state, and where everyone would do their best not to notice their dress or accents.

As in the case of Mills's military-industrial complex, there continue to be several grains of truth in the model. Certainly the professional classes are more powerful than they were. Yet this begs the question of which professions are in the ascendency and to what ends they deploy their power. It is also a legitimate question as to whether a meritocracy is invariably a good thing: Michael Young, in his influential book *The Rise of the Meritocracy*, saw drawbacks. (My own view is that a meritocracy should not be regarded as an ideal state of affairs, there being no such thing. Like democracy, it seems the least bad system.) In any event, the basic assumption – that as a meritocratic society was established, anti-elite reflexes and resentments would wither and fade away – has proved wrong. Meritocracy has stalled, not least because of egalitarian excesses in education. Far from diminishing, resentments against superior castes or canons have become built into our social structures, most notably in schools. But the main flaw in the theory of technological or professional elites is that, in common with many such utilitarian analyses, it omits the determining factor: culture.

Even more dated from today's perspective is the pessimistic left-wing counterpart of this liberal, optimistic image of open elites. According to this doggedly up/down view of society, the elites remain pretty much the same as they were: 'The extent of the political elite', wrote Tom Bottomore, a marxoidal man of the Left, in his generally instructive *Elites and Society*, 'is therefore relatively easy to determine: it will include members of the government and of the high administration, military leaders, and, in some cases, politically influential families of the aristocracy or royal house and leaders of powerful economic enterprises.'

Bottomore's book, still a standard text in higher education, was first published in 1964 and reissued in an updated version in 1993, from which the above quotation is taken. The striking thing about it is how little its vision of elites has changed in a third of a century. One can see why things looked like that in the early 1960s, but not any more.

So who and what are the elites today? On the face of it we seem to be left with little more than remnants of a bygone world. Yet society is by no means classless. There exists a powerful caste, helpfully identified in *A Class Act* by Stephen Pollard and Andrew Adonis as the 'super class', which has some of the characteristics of a modern elite. But its composition is loose and, though more meritocratic than its predecessors, it is less and less attracted to the exercise of public functions. Instead it is attracted to money, which is why the super class dominates the financial services industry, and to new sources of power, such as technology or the media. Influential as it is, the super class lacks the lineaments of an elite in the classic sense, precisely because it is so dissociated from government.

Nor do its members uphold or affect traditionalist norms of behaviour, or the values of an 'elitist' culture; they are far too worldly and hedonistic for that. A true elite incorporates an ideology, and apart from getting on in life it is hard to say exactly what the super class stand for. A banker earning £1,000,000 a year, with a mansion in Surrey and a wife jangling with jewellery with whom to make an annual outing to the opera, does not qualify for elite status. Even a paddock and ponies plus a hundred acres will not do the trick. He is merely a well-to-do man who feels obliged to take his wife to the opera once a year. The idea of a super class helps to explain the degeneration of the old elites, but it does little to help identify the new.

In politics, remnants of the old hierarchies exist. Almost a century after Michels noted how prominently the middle classes loomed in the socialist movement, we see a Labour Party that is led by the product of a private school and Oxford. Some of the traditional perquisites of power – the patronage, the nepotism, the political dynasties of the Right and Left – also remain. Political (and personal) cronies are appointed to the Lords, and well-born folk still find their way into the Commons. Peter Mandelson is the grandson of Herbert Morrison, Anthony Wedgwood Benn noisily abandoned his hereditary title but has just seen his son enter Parliament, Baroness Jay is the daughter-in-law of Jim Callaghan, and Francis Maude, David Heathcoat-Amory and Nicholas Soames are their fathers' sons. Equally clearly, the well-connected and well-to-do continue to have a greater say in the formation of public policy than the rest.

Yet somehow none of this seems to matter as much as it did. The main reason is the decline in the importance of politics. Why concern ourselves with the social pedigree or lack of it of our statesmen when all strive towards the sainted status of the middle classes, and when the very concept of 'statesmanship' has an antiquarian ring? In many people's eyes, notably her own, Mrs Thatcher qualified for this noble appellation, but somehow we do not expect another of her kind. Now the Cold War has gone and the economic changes she introduced have become accepted doctrine, the political function has become increasingly unheroic. History is not made by how much housing or invalidity benefit were under the Tories and how much under Labour, especially if they are much the same.

On the Right, much as our social reactionaries may lament it, there is no longer such a thing as a traditional governing class, and the final abolition of the hereditary element in the House of Lords is sweeping many old bones away. And much as the Left may pine for its old class enemy, it has gone or is going. The era of political elites in the archaic sense is tending to a close. We just don't think about them like that any more, even if that is how they prefer to think of themselves. Even the BBC has to be badgered by the Speaker into reporting their daily doings. The 'ruling elite' in politics is steadily declining into a quasi-anonymous administrative caste. Were it not for the colour of their rosettes it would be hard to tell one managerial pragmatist from the other.

A major reason for the eclipse of politics is the rise of market economics. A prime candidate for the succession would therefore seem to be the 'global elite' of businessmen – international conglomerates and the rest. Somehow the idea that our daily lives are manipulated this way and that by a handful of corporate interests seems too simple to be true. Except in certain areas, such as computer technology, the evidence is lacking, and even here it would be hard to see Bill Gates as the invisible hand controlling society. The source of his power lies not in his ability to influence governments (as his recent prosecution on anti-trust charges showed) but in the ability of depersonalized technology to change our lives. If Gates doesn't do it, someone else will.

Rupert Murdoch would be a more persuasive candidate for the role of hidden dictator. It is an awesome thought that it is possible to spend an entire day under his aegis. Such a day would begin with a breakfast show on Sky TV and a newspaper from the Murdoch stable, continue at a football match where the players may have been partially paid for by his stake in the club, include a visit to a movie made by Twentieth Century Fox and end with a bedtime book produced by his publishing arm, HarperCollins. Yet to think of Murdoch as the *numero uno* of the new elites is like blaming the Americanization of our society for all our ills: without willing collaborators in Britain – not to speak of willing consumers – it would not happen.

Also, there is nothing hidden about Murdoch. Lamentable as the effects of his populism may be on press or TV standards, he makes no bones about his commercial intent. Murdoch is that rare thing, an anti-elitist who means exactly what he says, and whom one could never imagine accepting a seat in the House of Lords. His aim is to make as much as he can by giving the public whatever they are deemed (or conditioned) to want, and he has no hesitation in putting other people's money where his mouth is. If everyone was as brazen about their intentions as Rupert Murdoch, British society would be a culturally poorer but far more honest place.

Media magnates can be accused of exploiting their holdings to interfere in the domestic democratic process, but for that very reason it is hard to categorize them as elites in the accepted sense. Global operators whose interests are scattered and who frequently reside outside the countries of their operations form an international citizenry, a category too abstract and too remote to qualify as members of the ruling caste in a particular country. This is not to deny their power and influence, though it is mostly exercised through local agents. A ruling stratum in the sense we have always understood the term must be a tangible presence, people we can see and hear.

Cultural and intellectual elites in the sense we have thought of them in the past are similarly hard to pinpoint. To qualify for the honour (or opprobrium) they would need to form cohesive groups standing at the apex of society, who enjoy power and prestige and whose values, though vocally contested, were generally dominant. Perhaps these people are there, but you would hardly know it. There comes a moment when what were previously seen as pinnacles of intellectual influence begin to appear as pockets of resistance against the prevailing culture. That point has long been reached. A pinnacle presupposes a base, and it is the base – an underlying understanding for what intellectuals are about – that is increasingly lacking. It is possible to have elite institutions without the members of those institutions constituting an elite in a functioning sense, and that seems where we are heading.

Private schools might appear to be an area where elitism flourishes. They have a hereditary element, and remain largely the preserve of the middle-to-upper-middle classes, the well-to-do and socially privileged. Mostly they provide a superior education, unavailable to the many, and continue to guarantee a high proportion of their pupils access to the best universities, good jobs and senior positions. But as will be discussed in a later chapter, the role in society of the products of the private school, as indeed those of top universities, is changing. For the moment it is enough to say that in cultural terms they are no longer a class apart. Elite is as elite does, and in their daily or professional lives the products of private schools are less likely than they were to uphold, even formally, values that could be described as above the norm. As with the super class identified by Pollard and Adonis, the approach is far more utilitarian.

A single statistic makes the point. Contrary to the image of public schoolboys grubbing away at dead languages, a mere 3 per cent of sixth formers at independent schools study the classics, and a large proportion of classics graduates go into financial services. The notion that the graduates of independent schools and top universities incarnate a certain idea of civic duty is similarly fanciful. Like everyone else, they live in an era of mass consumerism, and that is where most of them will make their money and their careers.

On the face of it, we would seem to be suffering from a dearth of elites in anything approaching the traditional meaning of the word: the 'flower of society' who combine wealth with power, and are seen as ruling in accord with a fixed set of beliefs (or self-serving prejudices if you will). Their apparent disappearance, and the difficulty of identifying a successor, confront our anti-elitists with a problem. Our neo-Machiavellians, who insisted that oligarchies merely changed their spots, face a problem too. Could it be that they were wrong, and that elites are finally receding from history, not just in the old sense but in every sense? Has society become a headless rider, all galloping hooves and foaming mouth, a mount without spurs or reins surging now in this direction, now in that, and going nowhere in particular?

In the past, things were clearer. When it came to identifying the ruling stratum in society, people could point the finger, knew where they stood. It mattered little whether their power was based on the divine right of kings or on politicians thrown up by the popular vote: each oligarchy in succession saw itself as the natural leader of the state and society, loudly proclaiming, and robustly defending, its right to rule. Now the claims of one elite to be the rightful heir to another are muted, the very idea that society is composed of the leaders and the led seen as anachronistic. Pareto's graveyard of aristocracies seems closed and barred. The tombs are full, the throne is empty. The crown of society's elites goes a-begging, and no one seems anxious to stake a claim.

One by one the usual suspects rule themselves out. Not us, say the remnants of the aristocracy. We are not so much an elite as victims: of caricature, of envy, of plebeian resentment. Nor us, laments the politician. Politics is perceived as a less dignified and ennobling pursuit than once it was, and our powers have shrunk as those of the market have expanded. Not me, says the general, somewhat nostalgically: where there are no large wars or imminent threats there can be no military elite worth the name. Not me, says the scientist or technocrat, wistfully: society does not appreciate us enough to cast us as its villains. Ditto, say the intellectuals, touchy as ever over their lack of status: canons of all kinds are out of fashion, and the idea that society is still dominated by something called a cultural elite is either a bad case of paranoia or a bad joke. Or us, says the Churchman with a celestial sigh: our congregations dwindle by the year, and the only time anyone takes notice of us today is when we debate homosexuality or woman priests. Us? say the trade unionists, sardonically. You are thirty years out of date.

The elite, in modern times, is always other people. Though perhaps we are looking in the wrong places? Rather than simply changing their spots, maybe our ruling castes have changed out of all recognition? Elaborating his theory of the circulation of elites, Mosca wrote:

What we see is that as soon as there is a shift in the balance of political forces – when, that is, a need is felt that capacities different from the old should assert themselves in the management of the state, when the old capacities, therefore, lose some of their importance or changes in their distribution occur – then the manner in which the ruling class is constituted changes also. If a new source of wealth develops in society, if the practical importance of knowledge grows, if an old religion declines or a new one is born, if a new current of ideas spreads, then, simultaneously, far-reaching dislocations occur in the ruling classes. (*The Ruling Class*)

Oligarchies may be inevitable, but at a time when the 'far-reaching dislocations' of which Mosca spoke have gone further than he and his generation could ever have expected, our oligarchs will assume a completely new aspect. The question we should be asking ourselves therefore is: if each age creates its distinctive elites, in a populist democracy, what will ours look like?

We think of elites as arrogant, aloof, contemptuous of ordinary humanity and anxious to keep as great a distance as possible between themselves and what the nineteenth century saw as 'the swinish multitude'. There would be little to be gained from adopting such attitudes today. Why should our new elites be figures of authority in the old sense? In a permissive, neo-liberal economic era, why not smiley, *laissez-faire* elites? The bread and circuses approach to power will surely work all the better in a consumer age, when public opinion and mass purchasing power, rather than social status, are the ultimate source of authority.

In the past, elites were prominent in our lives. But in a mass democracy how visible would they be? To judge by the difficulty of pinning them down, scarcely at all. For the first time in history we appear to be run by elites we find it hard to put a face to. Yet that too seems natural. Elites are seen as undemocratic, and it would be astonishing if they were to show their hand as openly as in the past – assuming, that is, that they know who they are and are conscious of their power. Anyone aspiring to a position of dominance in today's society would be inclined to give the appearance of doing the very opposite: wear the masses' clothes, affect their accents, hum their tunes and sympathize with their daily concerns, in the way that teachers attempt to put themselves on a par with their pupils and parents strive to enter into the spirit of their childrens' games.

Elites are thought of as settled, cumbrous, a deadening presence. Today they would be far less likely to form a point of stability. Rather they will take on the characteristics of their surroundings, chameleon-like. They will become evanescent, in constant flux – oligarchies whose influence depends on their ability to reflect the mood of the moment by catering to society's need for perpetual change. Should they fall behind the fashion they would risk becoming its victims: elites that are here one day, gone the next, to be replaced by what appear to be new faces but who turn out to be not so very different from those who went before. After a survey of the 300 most important powerholders in Britain, many of them new, the *Observer* (of 24 October 1999) concluded with relish: 'It is a fickle and cruel world indeed where in the space of twelve months more than 30 per cent of the most powerful people in the UK are relegated to the substitute's bench. To judge from the speed with which things change, we can expect similar changes next year.'

The *Observer's* 300 was, of course, an arbitrary figure. How numerous would our new elites be? Traditionally we conceive of them as castes and cliques who know one another socially and professionally and cooperate to advance their interests. Yet in a mass society, where blue blood is thinly distributed and family ties less constricting than they were, and where 'networking' takes place at all levels, there seems no reason why elites should be restricted to small circles or inbred groups. If we cling to Pareto's notion that society is invariably governed by a handful of powerful people, perhaps it is because its Machiavellian mystique intrigues us, or flatters our need for victimhood. In a mass society, where power is more widely distributed than in the past, why not massified elites?

Such elites would reflect a social body whose shape has altered in a literal sense. We still imagine society as a cone tapering swiftly to a pinnacle, where sit the dominant few. Yet that view is surely outdated, the geometry all wrong. Today the gradations of power and influence resemble a dome. But now it is no longer one that soars triumphantly to a peak: it is a dome that is ever broadening and flattening, so wide and flat that it tends towards the horizontal rather than the vertical. In other words, a structure where the highest level is at a minimal distance from the base, and where there is room for a multiplicity of leaders on the virtually levelled crown. It is no coincidence that the Greenwich Dome takes the form it does.

So our new elites would be numerically greatly extended, which suggests a dilution of quality. But to the modern eye that is not necessarily so. Smallness is a concept that goes with excellence and the ideal, and in the mass age the notion of the ideal is distrusted, for the obvious reason that it is not within the reach of everyone. In a massified society the ideal man is the average man, who becomes, in a sense, the superior man. We think of elites as being situated above us; professionally and financially, sometimes that may still be so. But in terms of their culture and capacities those who find themselves exercising power from the topmost reaches of our broad and flattened dome, though occasionally able men and women, may be not so far above the average level.

The point is important because it marks a departure from the optimistic, liberal idea that we are moving inexorably towards meritocracy. In seeking out our new elites we should not necessarily be looking for excellence, or for qualities that used to be seen as dividing 'the flower of society' from the rest, on some new measure of distinction. On the contrary, they are more likely to be men and women whose power springs from their ability to merge seamlessly with the mass. Their appeal in many cases will result from their capacities to promote the virtues of averageness, to rid the ordinary of its pejorative flavour and to raise it to the ideal. It follows that mediocrity rather than excellence could be a positive qualification for elite status.

Our modern elites could therefore be the very opposite of the ones we traditionally imagine. Michels may have been right about his iron law of oligarchy, yet in a modern democracy there is no reason why the oligarchy should be of a fixed size, that it should aspire to exist on an elevated cultural or intellectual plane, or even that the oligarchy's members should be exceptional individuals. Instead of flying high above society, the new elites could be floating on society's surface. Instead of being entrenched, they may well be rootless, not just 'moving with the times' but anticipating and promoting the movement of the times, so as to present themselves as ever changing, ever fresh. In other respects our new elites may not be so different from the old. Ruling oligarchies are not composed of poor, badly educated, badly connected people. Most will continue to be schooled above the norm (though that will be no proof of their intelligence), have money (though probably more income than capital) and be politically influential.

Seeking to describe the source of the power that regulated the society of his era, William Cobbett (1763–1835) talked of 'THE THING'. What he meant were the forces that, taken together, formed a kind of invisible despotism that conditioned the life of his time, in his view for the worse. To him THE THING seemed powerful, unyielding and irremovable precisely because it was so difficult to put a finger on. Yet wherever you went, you felt it. In 1835, the year of Cobbett's death, Tocqueville was discovering in America a different, democratic THING in the process of formation. Though equally hard to describe, he anticipated that it would be as pervasive as Cobbett's, and in *Democracy in America* he came up with a striking formulation. THE THING of the democratic future (Tocqueville did not use the word, but echoed the sense) would, he feared, be 'an anonymous despotism for which no one person would stand responsible'. Today it is clearer what he meant.

The anonymous despotism is populism. The word will feature frequently in this book. It is one that triggers warm emotions, often because of a confusion between the populist and the popular, so I shall clarify the difference as I see it. The popular represents the generality of taste or opinion. That in itself gives it no status. It can be enlightened or misguided, and however many crowd into the popular lobby on any given subject, each of us is allowed a view. For example, it is my belief that the public are misguided to enjoy Alan Bennett, or to demand, as until recently they did in their majority, to bring back hanging. Whereas (again in my view) the same public shows impeccable judgement in seeing *Have I Got News For You* as a funny TV show, or football as the supreme spectator sport. Others are at liberty to invert my preferences, and be keen rugbymen and hangers.

All I am saying – and it is strange to find oneself saying it at all – is that it is the absolute right of each of us to dissent as frequently and as loudly as we wish from the majority opinion of the moment, without being labelled elitists, just as it is the absolute right of others to go along with majority attitudes or beliefs without being dismissed as brainless automata. Even if society is 90 per cent in favour of this or that, that is no guarantee of its rightness or veracity. Popular taste and opinion are fallible for the same reason that individuals are fallible: because the people, like the individual, are human. And that is why populism, which means giving the public what they want (or are deemed to want), whatever they want, and telling them that it is good, is wrong in principle, for it implies that the majority are always right. Critical consumers know that a popular TV programme can be brilliant or imbecilic. The populist will insist that it is brilliant because it is popular.

The popular derives from the people, for good or ill. Populism, on the other hand, is something inflicted on them from above, with the aim of exploiting base or banal instincts for profit or position. In other words, populism is something that is done not *by* but *to* the people. Clearly the two things can merge or overlap, as when an affectedly folksy parliamentarian turns out to be a genuine football fan. And, of course, there are forms of commercial populism, such as weird coloured drinks or crass and vulgar films, that are pretty harmless. Clearly they are a form of exploitation but most people have better things to do than to get excited about it. The difference between commercial (i.e. private) and public crassness and vulgarity – e.g. in parliamentary debate, education or arts policy – is, however, a large one.

It is one thing for admen and entrepreneurs to appeal to low taste to make money; we can deplore it as much as we like, yet it is not strictly speaking their job to do otherwise. Nor is there any reason why their customers should not succumb, if that is their inclination and their wish. It is a quite different thing when an entire public culture, which takes its lead from on high, simultaneously defers to and exploits what it sees as mass opinion, in the way the new elites tend to do. When it permeates public affairs, the media and culture at every level, populism becomes arrogant and oppressive. It is arrogant because the scarcely veiled message is: 'We have money, the big numbers, modernity, the Zeitgeist, fashion and emotion on our side. So who are you, the individual, to criticize?' And it becomes oppressive because, in a very English way, that which is generally done quickly becomes custom, and that which is custom is swiftly transmuted into unwritten law, against which it is fruitless to protest.

At that point populism takes on a totalitarian aspect, not in the communist or fascist sense, but in the factual meaning of the term: a polity that operates in every field and which tolerates no rival loyalties. The right of the individual to dissent is not, of course, formally abolished, but dissent is discouraged by a suggestion that it would be presumptuous and undemocratic to fly in the face of the clearly expressed tastes and predilections of the majority. These are no abstract musings. Failure to conform to the populist imperative can cost people in politics, broadcasting, the press, education, academia, publishing or the arts their promotion or their jobs. Worse perhaps, previously independent-minded men and women find themselves involuntarily adapting to the demotic demands of the day.

But those who suffer most are the people. Populism as a public policy implies manipulation from above and a contempt for the manipulated. It is a perversion of democracy, the sickness of the age. When its attitudes and assumptions invade every sphere of our lives, demanding our allegiance and denouncing those who demur as snobs, elitists, or as alienated from the people, the democratic dictatorship against which Tocqueville warned – 'an anonymous despotism for which no one person would stand responsible' – is in danger of coming about. All in an amicable English way, naturally.

At the beginning of this chapter I cited the words of a self-proclaimed anti-elitist and her partner. Who were they, these scourges of privilege and authority, these partisans of the people? From her commanding demeanour the woman might have been a politician, a businesswoman or someone who had forged a successful career in the media. In fact she was all three: a senior executive in a company with interests in newspapers, television and popular entertainment of every kind. She came from a comfortable background, and had been educated at private school and at Oxbridge. A bright and forceful woman, she could have done well in a variety of other fields – the civil service, the law, the City. Instead she had decided (as Nicolas Berdiaev once accused those who go with the populist tide of doing) to 'make a career in the masses'.

In terms of power and prospects she had made an excellent choice. As an employee of a media enterprise making colossal profits she was a person of political influence, not just because politicians sought her views, but because she helped set the cultural climate within which politics operate. Her partner was a businessman in the entertainment industry who had recently made a tidy amount of money on a flotation, and whose views were also listened to avidly by government. Of his background I know nothing; I would guess it was not dissimilar to hers. Neither do I know which way they voted, though my hunch would be that it was Tory till the early nineties, then New Labour.

Listening to them, you felt a certain awe. The man and woman with strong feelings against elitism were a perfect sample of the source of power in modern times. Like contemporary society itself, their functions were loose, fluid, dispersed, infinitely adaptable. It was not hard to imagine their average day. One minute they might be sitting on a government quango examining reforms in education, the next on a company board deciding how to make a mid-market newspaper or TV show more appealing. Later it might be yet another government committee on how to increase the nation's invisible exports, or stimulate its creativity. Soon, no doubt, they would find themselves called upon to rejuvenate the governing bodies of theatres, publishers, art galleries, charities. Maybe one or both of our professional anti-elitists would end up in the House of Lords.

Their sense of authority and self-assurance was understandable, for together they were members of the contemporary THING. Machiavelli wrote that the only way the minority could rule the majority was by force or guile – the methods of the lion, or of the fox. Today we have the foxiest elite ever: one that rules in the people's name while preserving the lion's share of the power. For the first time in Western democratic history society is dominated by an elite of anti-elitists.

2

The Misunderstood Masses

The public always prefers to be reassured. There are those whose
job this is. There are only too many.

André Gide, *The Counterfeiters*

In this book I shall call the type of society where the new elites
hold sway an ultra-democracy. The term is open to instant
misunderstanding, not to say misrepresentation, so let me be
clear what I mean. I am not suggesting that the rule of the people
has gone too far. I use *ultra* in its true meaning of 'beyond',
rather than in the sense of extreme. (The pigment ultra-marine
is so called because it came from beyond the seas – Persia and
Afghanistan – not because it is extremely blue.) An ultra-
democracy is not therefore a society where democracy is
extended to the limit – obviously a desirable state of affairs. It
is one where democracy is denatured by taking the notion of the
sovereignty and equality of the people to seductive, demagogic
lengths, and where the debasement of genuine democratic values
is encouraged from above. Ultra-democracy, in other words, is
anti-democratic.

Democracy elevates, ultra-democracy lowers. Democracy
encourages freedom of aspiration and the autonomy of the
individual within society. Ultra-democracy portends new forms
of control, as the people are regimented into cohorts of mass
men and women, the better to homogenize their appetites and
satisfy their tastes. It promises a classless society freed from

hierarchies in which the desires of the individual are given their weight, and delivers the opposite: a society ruled by class consciousness elevated into a system and directed from above in malleable herds. 'Giving the people what they want' implies a top–down motion: there is one who gives and there is one who receives. The choice, ultimately, is made from above, for it is there that the selection available is decided. There is therefore no contradiction between the growth of ultra-democracy and the emergence of the new elites, indeed one involves the other.

Before examining our new captains of society more closely it seems sensible to establish who are the other ranks. If the elites are no longer those we traditionally imagined, how can we be sure what constitutes the masses? The subject is a touchy one. It is a curiosity of contemporary society that, while it seems natural to debate the identity of the elite, to allude to the existence of a mass is seen as indelicate. For reasons it would take a social psychologist to explain, 'the masses' is a term not much favoured in mass societies. The very words can cause bristles to rise on ultra-democratic napes and, of course, we never think of or refer to ourselves in these terms. People will confess to (or boast of) being upper-middle class, take a residual pride in being working class or admit to membership of the dismal middle. The one thing it would never occur to them to do is to present themselves as a member of the elite or of the mass; to describe oneself as a mass man or woman would be as unthinkable as to assert that 'the elite, *c'est moi*'.

Yet there is no escaping social reality. However much the meaning has been changed by history, and however inconvenient it may be to our social sensitivities to acknowledge the fact, the masses, like the elite, continue to exist. C. Wright Mills, a healthy-minded liberal, showed no queasiness on the matter. 'The idea of a mass society', he wrote in *The Power Elite*, 'suggests the idea of an elite of power.' The same is clearly true in reverse: elites of power, new or old, presuppose a mass.

Our reluctance to use the term outside specified contexts is revealing. Obviously we have a fear of sounding snobbish, but there is a deeper reason. The idea of large numbers of people acting in a predictable and malleable manner brings us face to face with truths we would prefer not to think about. Democracy has its etiquette, its little politenesses. As in everyday life, some things are best left unsaid. Politicians, businessmen and media folk think in terms of mass men and women, and could describe them down to the colour of their socks, but for them to speak the words would be professional suicide. They would be seen as an expression of contempt, uncomfortably close to the nineteenth-century notion of the mob. Yet we need some means of designating the obvious, which is why we resort to euphemisms such as Middle England, Mondeo man or 'your average punter'; expressions which, unlike mass man, retain a wry residue of human warmth.

Ideally we might prefer to expunge 'the masses' from our democratic lexicography. If we do not like the idea of being governed by an elite, how much more vexatious to be thought of as members of the mass? But to do away with the expression altogether would not be easy, for in limited contexts, like 'elite', it remains in positive use. 'Mass society' can be made to seem a good or a bad thing: good in the sense that we are all in it together, and have certain cooperative instincts when it comes to welfare or resistance to aggression; bad when it implies a civilization reduced to automatons. We warm to the expression when it denotes righteousness in a good cause (mass solidarity, mass support, mass indignation against repellent crimes) but are fearful of its insect-like associations.

In permitted senses populist elites use the word routinely and without embarrassment. Politicians like nothing so much as 'a mass audience', commercial interests strain to reach 'mass markets', film or pop stars delight in their 'mass appeal', while cultural officialdom does its best to encourage 'mass participation'. There is a large dose of hypocrisy here. Those who would be the first to object to the whole idea of 'the masses' as reactionary in a modern society are happy to resort to an identical concept when the multitudes in question are people whose cash or good opinion are coveted by such as themselves. At that point mass impulses and mass preferences become sanctified, the purest expression of democracy and individual choice.

We cannot have things both ways. If there is such a thing as a mass audience or mass market it follows that there must be such a thing as a mass, with massified tastes, masses of money to dispose of and with the tendencies towards mass behaviour described by students of crowd psychology over generations. From the classic *Extraordinary Popular Delusions and the Madness of Crowds* written by Charles Mackay in the mid nineteenth century, to Elias Canetti's *Crowds and Power*, published in 1930, few thinkers have been in any doubt about the phenomenon. Mackay announced his purpose as 'to collect the most remarkable instances of those moral epidemics which have been excited, sometimes by one cause and sometimes by another, and to show how easily the masses have been led astray, and how imitative and gregarious men are, even in their infatuations and crimes'. Canetti described the four main attributes of the crowd in simple but evocative terms: 'The crowd wants to grow ... Within the crowd is equality ... The crowd loves density ... The crowd needs a direction ...'

All this would seem self-evident, yet qualms about acknowledging the existence of mass attitudes and mass behaviour remain. The new elites, for obvious reasons, are amongst the most reluctant. Even as the power of celebrities, from cooks to royalty, Diana to Delia Smith, to attract mass followings swells to awesome proportions, and a single TV soap commands the allegiance of a third or more of the population, they lose no opportunity to refer to the growing diversity of our culture. Politicians especially are fond of describing society as composed of clusters of individuals – niche markets, specialized tastes, opinion groups and the rest – even as they address it as if it were a moronic multitude.

Pluralism is a modish concept, scientists are not immune to fashion, and they too join in the hymn to diversity. As geneticists unravel the determinating patterns of our make-up, which suggest that our choices in life may be rather less than we had hoped, in a sort of compensatory emphasis sociobiologists have taken to celebrating the infinite plurality of nature. Their reassurances do not invariably reassure. The American sociobiologist E. O. Wilson, a brilliant and often persuasive writer, celebrates pluralism in the natural world, and by extension that of our own. This would be encouraging, except that he is especially good at describing the army-like conformity of insect life. The question is, does a series of species, each behaving in a rigidly predictable manner, add up to a plurality?

The same contradiction is apparent in upbeat talk about a growing diversity in lifestyles, notably in the media, where the more we are told that we are witnessing a revolution in choice, the more the programmes or newspapers look uncannily alike. Sceptics will rightly wonder how it is possible to assert that society is characterized by a healthy pluralism at a time when the cultures of different races and social strata appear to be relentlessly converging. Anyone who doubts this should try watching Chinese or Indian television (Indian TV especially), or measure the contents of Sunday newspapers with supposedly different political philosophies against one another. The novelist Tim Parks has provided a convincing explanation of what is happening. Speculating about the future of literature, he recently wrote: 'We can expect an extraordinary variety of genre and apparent eclecticism, but with an underlying conformity of sentiment and vision.' As in literature, so in life.

Ambivalence about mass man runs deep. Advanced democracies recoil from this undignified and somewhat threatening creature even as they go out of their way to manufacture him, to celebrate him, to exploit him – and perhaps soon to clone him. With the ambivalence goes a certain nervousness, and whenever the predilections of mass man are in question, cant is the norm. In public, he is portrayed as the repository of every virtue. In private, the contempt of the politician for the electorate whose wishes he gives every appearance of venerating, of the celebrity performer for the audience he vows is the best he has ever had, of the pop star for his shrieking nymphets, the editor for the cultural levels of his readers or the businessman for the customers whose taste and discrimination he cannot praise enough, can be imposing to behold.

So who exactly constitute this mass in modern times? Mentally we consult our up/down, Left/Right compass. No more delicate piece of machinery has been devised. Whatever the matter in hand, we can instantly check our coordinates to ensure we are pointing in the approved direction. Never mind that society has shifted on its axis, that the needle is all awry, and that – as we have seen in the case of the new elites – the compass markings no longer make sense. Never mind that henceforth north can mean south, or that Left and Right are no longer opposites. We have a vague notion that the whole thing is defective, but are prepared to risk getting lost with it because we are damned sure we shall be lost without it. Deprived of their up/down, Left/Right compass, the English would literally not know what to think.

A quick check reveals the apparently obvious: that the elites and the masses lie at opposite poles. So it used to be. In premodern times the distinction between them was starkly and shockingly clear. Now that the social ranks have closed, and the elite have taken to camouflaging themselves, like tanks in the undergrowth, in the colours of the mass, it is far from simple to know where one ends and the other begins. The problem is that old ideas about the masses are hard to turn around. Historically they were seen as something submissive and inert; acted upon rather than acting, except when they were driven to revolt. But today they no longer denote the destitute, the dispossessed, the hungry, 'the working class' or the incipiently revolutionary.

In Britain, with its nostalgic mindset and tenacious conventions, it is hard to discuss these things freely. To this day the categories of debate remain those set by *Culture and Society* by Raymond Williams. Published over forty years ago, it is still seen as applicable to contemporary life. In fact, its highly politicized approach to social and cultural themes, like the flimsy, two-dimensional decor of the fifties, is badly out of date. One can see why its appeal grew in the sixties, but not why it is so frequently invoked today – unless, that is, we are bent on reliving the sixties. To read it now is to feel that you are being constantly asked the rather heavily loaded question of whether you are for or against the common man. The trouble is that the common man has evolved rather faster than Williamsite thinking.

Williams's view of the masses was, of course, conditioned by his left-wing politics (he had once been a supporter of Stalin). Yet even allowing for the fact that he was writing in an era of far greater social division and class antagonism than today, his analysis of this key concept in twentieth-century life is extraordinarily blinkered. He begins, reasonably enough, by suggesting that to some minds the term 'the masses' had become a new word for 'the mob'. Mass production, mass meetings, mass action – all such expressions had helped to give the term a negative coloration. Hence, he argues, its unfair connotations of low tastes, fickleness and gullibility. Hence too the fear that mass thinking, mass suggestion and mass prejudice would one day prove a threat to democracy. Williams was also right to note that the very term 'mass democracy' can be either an observation or a prejudice. As an observation it is a statement of fact, of the kind which flags up problems. As a prejudice it suggests that the speaker is not interested in thinking about or solving those problems: 'what is being questioned is not mass democracy, but democracy'.

All this is reasonable and persuasive. It is when Williams begins to appeal to our emotions, suggesting that none of us wants to think of him or herself as the man or woman in the street, that things start going wrong. It is obviously true that we prefer not to think of ourselves in these terms, but that has no bearing on whether or not the man in the street – mass man – exists. People do not like to think of themselves as heathens, but technically an increasing majority of the British are. Nor do they like the idea of being labelled tax-dodgers, yet in small ways, usually to do with VAT, most of them are that as well. This touch of sentimentalism alerts us to the fact that Williams's case is heading in a dangerous direction. Sure enough, suddenly the chain of logic snaps and the entire argument about the masses goes hurtling into an abyss. In *Culture and Society* the sequence goes: 'Who are the masses? In practice, and in this context, they can hardly be other than the working people ... Masses = majority cannot be glibly equated with masses = mob ... The masses are always the others, whom we don't know and can't know ... Masses are other people. There are in fact no masses.'

The leap Williams has made is extraordinary. To protect the working class from being labelled 'the masses' with malign intent, he has allowed himself to be driven into the absurd position of saying that there are no masses at all. It is clear that he reached this conclusion not by spontaneous analysis, but by reaction against the conservative critics of his day, who he believed saw mass culture as inferior, the culture of the mob. There is an element of almost childish stubbornness in Williams's stance, like those right-wingers who contend with a straight face, in response to criticism about royalty being out of touch, that the monarchy identifies with ordinary people far more closely than its critics. He could easily have made his point about the dangers of equating the working classes with the masses, then proceeded to define what we mean by the masses in a more modern and more truthful way. Instead, intent on trumping conservative critics, he takes his argument to grotesque extremes. A better instance of the danger of becoming locked into up/down, Left/Right thinking than Williams's casual abolition of the masses, and presumably of mass society with them, is difficult to imagine.

The masses are not an abstract category whose existence can be called into question by professors. In industrialized societies and evolved democracies in the second half of the twentieth century 'the masses' mean, quite simply, humanity in the mass. The one thing Williams was right about was to reject our tendency to see the masses as the working class, or as other people, which of course they are not. The masses are ourselves. Only when they are released from their pokey-minded, party-political prison can the relationship between the masses and the elites be understood. The key is to break with the past and to look at them more conceptually, which in this instance also means more practically. To this end I will attempt a thought experiment with Raymond Williams, designed to disprove his contention that the masses – and by extension mass man – do not exist.

Had our professor laid aside his studies for a day, and spent the morning at a sale of 'Fine and Important' old master paintings at Sotheby's, then watched a TV quiz show, live, then assisted at a football match followed by a riot, then dropped in on a snooty cocktail party, before finishing the evening at an expensive night club, he might have come to see the masses for what they are.

At the Sotheby's sale he would have been struck, and somewhat repelled, by the ripple of applause that spread round the saleroom when, after a tense bout of bidding, a particularly fine and important painting went under the hammer for five times its estimate. Whence his distaste? Because the reaction of the well-heeled, socially select audience to the unexpectedly large sum earned by the picture was profoundly vulgar. Every bit as vulgar, in fact, as the oohs and aahs of a very different audience when the prize-money in the quiz show he was later to see was announced by a succulent blonde – the type of blonde who somehow enjoys an umbilical attachment to money and who, transferred from thigh boots and leather skirt into cashmere jumper and pearls, might not have looked totally out of place in Sotheby's. Vulgarity, the professor could only have concluded, is no monopoly of any social class, but one of those deplorable tendencies so frequently displayed by humanity in the mass.

Proceeding to his afternoon football match and subsequent riot the professor would have experienced mass phenomena in the more vigorous form of crowd dynamics ('the crowd needs a direction'). Escaping shaken but untrampled by mounted police, he would then change from cap and scarf into sober suit and tie for his cocktail party. Feeling rather out of it amongst the nobs and snobs, he would have liberty to observe crowd dynamics of a not totally different kind: high society guests vying with one another through their dress, speech or behaviour to show that they were each at least the equal of the other ('within the crowd is equality').

As for the expensive night club, where the professor was dragged by a society hostess who thought him quaint, he would have been struck by the way the gilded clientele ogled the stripped-down women in the cabaret and laughed at the comedians' obscenities very much as working men (and now working women too) were apt to do at pub floor shows, drinking too much as they watched and tapping their feet to a not dissimilar rhythm. Having had a glass too many, he might even have done some ogling and giggling himself. Togetherness is contagious, pretty much irrespective of who and where you are ('the crowd loves density'). At the end of his exhausting but enlightening day the professor would have fallen into a profound sleep, though not before lamenting the foibles and excesses of humanity in the mass – weaknesses to which it could hardly have succumbed had mass humanity not existed.

In consumer societies of the late twentieth century, mass man exists independently of his or her social or economic status. The predisposition to low taste, vulgar behaviour or crowd imperatives is there to be appealed to in every one of us. Herd behaviour can be unpretty, at whatever social level and however large or small the herd. Mass men and women are classless, not in the sense that they do not belong to distinct economic castes, but that they share qualities (and not exclusively negative qualities) that transcend those castes. That is what converts them from individuals into a mass.

The classifications used by advertisers are the most contemporary illustration of the point. When they attempt to target such and such a product at the 'ABC1s' they are bundling together huge swathes of the population. The gamut runs from Eton- and Oxford-educated Lords through polytechnic-educated engineers to self-employed plumbers who, rare as they are and valuable as their skills may be, have not by and large enjoyed a higher education. The point is that all may be tempted by hair-restorants or laddish magazines, just as their female counterparts may be lured into spending hundreds of pounds on grossly overpriced and completely redundant cosmetics.

As for their cultural predilections, it is not hard to envisage every one of them, from plumbers to hereditary peers, being persuaded into giving over many hours of their leisure to a TV costume drama series. All that is required is that the carriages should crunch audibly enough on the drive, that the stars look lovely in period dress and that the whole should evoke memories of another England: an England where the masses (as then conceived) had the decency to stay largely out of sight, and where no vulgar admen existed to exploit mass sensibilities (as they have now become) by lumping diverse social classes together as ABC1s in the crude and deplorable manner they do today.

It should hardly be necessary to point out that an expensively educated member of the upper classes can be as susceptible to mass thinking as a street sweeper scarcely schooled at all. When remnants of the aristocracy, or more often aspirants to that class, privately lament that people are not as deferential as they used to be towards such as themselves, or that the lower orders have become horribly 'chippy', they are displaying great vulgarity of mind. Their social preconceptions are as vain as they are stupid, and in this respect they can be more vulgar than street sweepers, whose grip on reality may be closer.

Most prejudices, such as the notion that all politicians are crooks or that all homosexuals are perverts – views that are widely distributed amongst both street sweepers and aristocrats, not to speak of intermediate levels – are evidence of mass thinking. Believing that celebrities are necessarily people of interest or accomplishment by virtue of their celebrity – the sort of people aristocrats would be happy to be photographed alongside for a gossip column in *Hello* magazine, and for whom the street sweeper would feel privileged to cleanse the pavement on which they trod – is another obvious instance where mass credulity operates independently of social status.

There is no better example of mass thinking than snobbery itself. It operates at every social level, and its etymology is famously revealing. Let us never forget that this now internationalized word (snob in Russian, snob in Italian, snob in French) was a British invention: it got its name from the affectations of boys at public schools who, though non-aristocrats – *sine nobilitate*, hence snob – behaved as if they were. Snobbery is a mass phenomenon because it reflects a widespread tendency to judge people in terms of status, social caste and external show, irrespective of merit: it is mass in the sense of thinking in group categories, rather than individual virtue, and mass in the sense of being ordinary. The reason that snobbery in all its forms – the populist snobbery of the new elites included – ranks amongst the worst of human failings is because it is vulgarity of the soul.

In an ideal world there would, of course, be no masses. 'Civilization exists', wrote Georges Bernanos, 'precisely so that there may be no masses but rather men alert enough never to constitute masses.' It is an agreeable thought, but in such a world there would also be no common tendency to sin or to behave morally. For there are good sides to mass man as well as bad, and when it comes to more positive aspects of his tastes or behaviour, for example the quality and vitality of certain forms of popular culture, today Professor Williams, champion of the common man, would be seen as bludgeoning down an open door. No person of taste and intelligence denies that popular culture can achieve a high aesthetic level and appeal to every section of the population (i.e. humanity in the mass). Examples include the lyrical simplicity of The Beatles, the wittiest sitcoms, the best of Dylan's songs or Pelé's pass to Carlos Alberto that Eric Cantona saw as being up there with Rimbaud. But as sensible persons also know, the overwhelming majority of popular culture, pop music especially, is meretricious ephemera – a defect which does not always prevent it from appealing to humanity in the mass. And it goes without saying that when its achievements are measured against its pretensions, much 'high culture', literary or artistic, can be pretty rubbishy too. There is no shortage of rotten plays, ill-written 'literary' novels or infantile art. The tendency to counterpose a false idea of the masses to a false idea of the elites deforms the current debate about whether society is 'dumbing down' or 'wising up', and will be touched upon in a later chapter.

Up/down, Left/Right thinking is our national cross. It oppresses our politics and our culture, and to unburden ourselves of its weight we must look abroad. Almost thirty years before Williams's book appeared, the Spanish humanist Ortega y Gasset moved the discussion about the masses to a higher plane. It is a measure of Williams's parochialism that *Culture and Society* does not even mention him, even to dismiss him. Yet it is impossible to discuss mass man and the mass society without reference to Ortega's position.

Ortega (1883–1955) has long been in and out of fashion, mostly out. It was his fate to be admired at the wrong time, often for the wrong reasons. Praise from suspect right-wing quarters or from snobs has tarnished his reputation. He is one of those writers whose work was tussled over by Left and Right, then cast aside, like a bone abandoned by angry dogs who have found something new to fight over. For those who wish to know, his main message is still clear on the page, and its relevance is increasing. Ortega was to the masses what Pareto or Michels were to the elites: an annunciator of what now seem self-evident truths who was reviled for his pains. (Their fate is not confined to conservatives: the same is true of certain of Marx's analyses of nineteenth-century capitalism, which retain their validity to this day, and of many pages of Gramsci, Adorno and Marcuse.) The fact that some of Ortega's thinking, like that of Pareto, now appears illiberal and outdated is not in question. Yet contrary to caricature, the purpose of his great work *The Revolt of the Masses* was not to sound the alarm over the insurrection of the underdog. Though a conservative thinker, he was a democrat, and did not believe in anything so antediluvian as the congenital inferiority of the working class. His detachment from conventional political thinking allowed him to see the masses for what they are:

The division of society into masses and select minorities is not, then, a division into social classes, but into two kinds of men, and it does not depend on hierarchically superior or inferior classes, on upper classes and lower classes ... We must be careful not to think of the masses as the labouring classes: the masses are the average man.

The 'select minorities' he defines as those who demand more of themselves than others, 'even when the demands are unobtainable'. Mass man he sees as someone who does not value himself, for good or ill, by any particular criterion. It is a rough and ready distinction. An unaspiring person, for all his or her ordinariness, is not any less of a human being. Nor am I convinced by Ortega's subsequent argument (though in full it is subtler than it sounds) that in order to form part of a worthwhile culture it is necessary to detach oneself from the multitude. If that were true there would be no popular culture of high worth, which is manifestly not the case. Nevertheless, the basic point – that the masses are the average man and not the social underdog – stands. It is a message that deserves to be engraved on English hearts.

Our reluctance to take the point is understandable. To see the mass as the median line, rather than the lower, at once destroys the false antithesis on which our discussion about the elites and the masses is traditionally based. The implications of adjusting to reality would be intolerable. Consciences could no longer be warmed in ritual denunciations of elites, or in the refracted glow of the masses' virtue. Romantic notions about the wisdom/innocence/vitality/spiritual purity of those below society's salt would instantly dissolve: for to assert the ethical superiority of the masses would merely be to celebrate the glories of the average man, i.e. of humankind as a whole. Compared to what other humanity? would then become the question. With no masses to look down on in satisfaction, patronizing pop culture, good or poor, a speciality of egalitarian elites, would make no sense. For if the mass man were merely the average man, and the elites were not so far above him, they would be in danger of condescending to themselves.

You can see why we cling to dear old Raymond Williams for comfort. A truthful view of men and women in the mass would throw the entire English social game out of kilter. All the fun and ferocity would go from the debate if we were deprived of our traditional up/downery and forced to think. Like TV sets that can only receive a new signal by the addition of a new box of tricks, mindsets would have to be radically readjusted. Few are ready to go to such trouble and most prefer the old programmes. It is easier to deal in familiar, emotive categories than to face society as it is: a heterogeneous mixture of individuals who fall into broad social bands but who retain fundamental characteristics in common. As Flaubert was fond of saying, it is always hard work depicting the commonplace, and in Ortega's mass man there is more than a suggestion of the *homme moyen sensuel.*

His importance in the context of this book is not just that he gave a more truthful diagnosis of that much-abused word, the masses. He also foresaw the dangers of a malignant populism more clearly than many before or since. In particular he anticipated the emergence of societies where demagogy would be institutionalized and where the tenets of anti-elitism would become instruments of control. As a cultural conservative he was inclined to stress the dark side of the twentieth-century soul. For Ortega, man in the mass was potentially anti-rational, anti-intellectual, anti-culture, someone who, in his chilling phrase, wants 'to have done with discussion'. His most brilliant prediction concerned the perils of crowd psychology in mass societies of the Nazi type (his book appeared in 1930). Mass man was ripe for exploitation by unscrupulous leaders who would play on his most negative characteristics: 'In the guise of syndicalism and fascism there appears for the first time in Europe a type of man *who does not want to give reasons, or even to be right*, but who is determined to impose his opinions' (Ortega's italics). Hitler, it goes without saying, was mass man at his most inhuman.

No doubt it seems a long way from the racism and corporatist socialism of the Nazis to the soft-bellied populism of inverted elites today, whom it would be fanciful to portray as little Hitlers. The link lies in the exaltation of mass man as the norm, and in the temptation of those in authority to exploit his tendency to behave as a creature of sentiment rather than reflection: a man already certain of his likes and dislikes and who wants 'to have done with discussion'. His outstanding feature is that, not only is he unabashed by his ordinariness, he is determined his tastes should prevail everywhere: 'The commonplace mind, knowing itself to be commonplace, has the assurance to proclaim the rights of the commonplace and to impose them wherever it will.' No better summation of the debilitating effects of populist democracies can be imagined.

A society that has an outdated understanding of who are its elites and who are its masses is incapable of forming an objective view of itself. Forever it will be doomed to re-fight old wars in radically changed conditions. In Kierkegaard's words, this is 'the result of having fought for centuries against Kings, Popes and the powerful, and having looked upon the people and the masses as something holy. It does not occur to people that historical categories change . . .' The realization that there is nothing holy about the masses – how can there be, if the masses are ourselves? – opens our eyes. Only then can we respond critically though with sympathy, rather than sentimentally and self-interestedly, to what we see around us. Only then can we think and talk about human affairs, society, art or politics, not in up/down categories, but on the level. Only then would people be free to say positive things about mass culture without appearing ingratiating, or to explain why they think so much of it is trash without being accused of snootiness. Only then could the individual argue against majority opinion in the interests of the majority, without the ready-gummed label of elitism being slapped on him or her. An honest view of the mass society might even help rid us of our parasitical elites. In status-obsessed Britain, talking on the level would be more than a huge relief. It would be a national liberation.

3

A Populist Oligarchy

O Demos, how can there ever be a man
who loves you as dearly as I? . . .
Vouchsafe to blow your nose, and clean
your fingers on my hair.

Paphlagon in *The Knights*, Aristophanes

It is time to put more flesh on the bones of our egalitarian
elites. Superficially they may seem no more than a new breed of
populist snob. Inverted snobbery has a long tradition and – by
definition – a distinguished pedigree. 'I rather like bad wine,'
said Mr Mountchesney in Disraeli's *Sybil*. 'One gets so bored
with good wine.' Today Mountchesney's spiritual heirs would
be insisting how much they adore downmarket TV or discovering themselves late in life to be ardent football fans. Their
enthusiasms are tiresome because they are often hypocritical,
their purpose less to identify with democratic values than to
emphasize the distance between themselves and the victims of
their condescension. The inverted snob, usually, is a snob *tout
court*. Honest arrogance can be preferable to the Mountchesney
style: when a wine waiter recommended a bottle to Randolph
Churchill on the grounds that it was popular, Churchill was not
pleased: 'What makes you think', he shot back, 'I want to drink
anything popular?'

Inverted snobs merely irritate. Inverts of elitism are a more
powerful and far more damaging breed, whose purpose goes far

beyond a little social or gastronomic slumming. They are not idealists or romantics who immerse themselves in The People as something holy, like the faithful in the Ganges. For them the masses are a natural force which, suitably harnessed, can be made to generate money, power or position. And they are not amateurs at the game. Our modern elites do not dabble in populism, as the old elites were occasionally obliged to do, to round a tricky corner: they have erected populism into a profession, a strategy, a system.

In sketching in some faces on our anti-elite elites, for the moment I shall leave aside the obvious candidates: the rock stars and sundry celebrities. We shall come to them. Too close a focus at this point on the frothier examples of the genre would run the risk of distracting attention from egalitarian elites in their institutional form. The first thing to be said of them is that, although New Labour and its acolytes are prominent amongst them, they are not confined to a single political tendency. The left-wing newspaper editor and right-wing TV mogul are equally intent on pleasuring the masses, about whom they will hear no ill. Consequently there is little to choose between their products. That is why, for all the alleged ideological difference between them, the *Daily Mirror* looks and reads not unlike the *Sun*. It is also why it is increasingly hard to distinguish between BBC and commercial television.

Nor are the new elites confined to a single social stratum. The most successful amongst them frequently come from favoured backgrounds, though their origins, like their functions, can be highly diverse. They can be aristocrats or meritocrats, upper-middle or lower class, or people of working-class roots who convert their social origins into a profession. Even royalty, as we shall see, are not excluded. In that sense at least our new ruling caste is highly democratic, and access is open to all who believe in, or are willing to pay lip service to, the populist creed.

Many of those who fit the mould of inverted elites would be surprised to find themselves referred to in this way. Few take kindly to being described as forming part of a power elite, fewer still as standing on their heads. Those I have in mind occupy important positions in politics, education, the media, culture and commerce. Together they form a populist oligarchy whose power and influence extend throughout society. Oligarchy is a dated word, and I use it in an updated sense. In the past it meant government by the like-minded few. To adapt it to the mass society, with its multiple sources of decision, its scope must be expanded, and the oligarchy I have in mind is both numerous and widely spread.

Traditional elites maintained their coherence and ensured their perpetuation through a nepotistic system of schools, clubs, clans, regiments, officers' messes, Inns of Court, cultural canons, social contacts and the rest. Egalitarian elites operate on a similar basis. Parliamentary populists, the regiments of like-minded executives in the mass media, the cartels of a commercialized culture, the celebrity circuit, quangos, cronies, literary and artistic cliques, cultural apparatchiks and the free-masonry of educationists – though more numerous and fluid than in the past, the power centres of populism interconnect at vital points, and are no less exclusive and intolerant of outsiders than their historical predecessors. (Though they can be less inclined to stick together. The case of Peter Mandelson – the pearly prince of the new elites – is instructive in this regard. Here is a man who has made his career in the media, only to be eaten alive by the very people who helped to create and sustain his personal myth. Lacking the rigid caste system that bound the old elite together, the new elites can develop cannibalistic tendencies: when they are not feeding off popular gullibility they are feasting off each other.)

Though they can and do operate across different professions, it would be a mistake to see them as conspirators who have come together to dominate the system. And distasteful as their activities can be, it would be wrong automatically to ascribe malign motives to individual members of our populist oligarchy.

Despite a tendency to affect values which can sometimes be the opposite of the ones they practise or believe, notably in culture and education, the new elites are not all imposters or uniformly ill-intentioned. Some – the obsequious politician, the vulgarizing media executive, the cloyingly people-friendly tycoon – may be cynics, careerists or profiteers. Others – the cultural official earnestly 'democratizing the arts', or the chief education officer implementing a rigorously anti-elitist policy in his dismally underperforming schools – see themselves as agents of social progress, analogous to liberal-minded nineteenth-century patricians. Still others are conformists, mere drifters with the demotic tide, whose overriding concern is to secure their income and position: the jobsworths, as it were, of the new elites.

The publisher who culls her list in search of what is described as a wider readership may simply be pre-empting a takeover bid which could cost her her job, or going along with the demands of her new bosses when a takeover is successful. The senior BBC man who adapts his programmes to 'a younger and more varied audience' is vilified for vulgarization, when he may simply be reacting to the latest ratings and the popular mood. The vice chancellor whose zeal in widening access crosses the line into positive discrimination, with the risk of downgrading his univer-sity, is more likely to be motivated by the pursuit of a quiet life than by leftist dogma. (Also, perhaps, like the BBC executive, by a tremor or two of guilt and fear.)

Consciously or otherwise, passively or energetically, by cyni-cal calculation or by demotic drift, such people are 'making a career in the masses'. And what other career is there, the ambitious might ask? On a detached view of contemporary society, they are right. You no longer become rich and powerful by pandering to princes, but you can become very rich and exceedingly powerful by affecting to make princes of the people. And whereas in former times you might have been scorned for being a base flatterer of monarchs, insinuating oneself into the affections of the masses can be so contrived as to acquire a moral dimension. At their most benign, populist elites promise a degree of equality that, with the best will in the world, they are unable to deliver. And, of course, the best will in the world is frequently lacking. The new elites are prone to describing themselves as committed egalitarians, but the problem with egalitarians is that they are so rarely on the level.

The French utopian socialist Francois Fourier (1772–1837) imagined a world where every threatening or disagreeable thing became the contrary of itself. Not only was everyone kind enough to cooperate with everyone else, lions became anti-lions, cuddly and docile as lambs, beetles became uncreepy and so forth. In similar fashion modern elites seek the favours of the people by presenting themselves as the opposite of what they are. This denial of being itself, this cross-dressing in the masses' clothes, begins in politics.

The last two British administrations have both projected themselves as anti-government. The Conservatives talked about getting government off the people's backs, while New Labour insists that it is the people who are in charge. (Their habit of describing everything as the people's this or the people's that is a measure of the earnestness of the pretence, as well as their indifference to history; clearly they are deaf to the unfortunate echoes of regimes which, only eleven years ago, still existed.) To that end the Government gives the impression of seeking guidance and wisdom from the masses before taking a step, through opinion polls, focus groups and other processes of consultation. At the same time, denunciations of the arrogance of elites are forever on its lips. In the 1997 election Tony Blair's preface to the Labour Party manifesto assailed 'an elite at the top increasingly out of touch with the rest of us'. An appealing sentiment – we all like to believe that there is someone up there doing us down – but those two little letters 'us' give the game away. The private school and Oxford graduate and (at the time) prime minister-in-waiting does not confine himself to seeking social justice for others. He insists, in fine Fourier style, on being the opposite of what he is. In populist democracies the lions rub up against the masses with lamb-like noises.

In power, the disguise becomes pitiably transparent. The instincts of our professional anti-elitists can be remarkably authoritarian, and when it comes to getting its message across the Government behaves in highly traditional ways. While inclining its head before The People, it does everything in its power to influence their opinions, so as to condition in advance the views of an electorate it shows itself most anxious to consult. The wheedling tone of ministers is an example of the same phenomenon, even when their actions – especially in the economy – are rather less gentle than their personal styles. As language and demeanour become as important as substance, demotic modes of debate and expression, once the province of the cruder populists, become the norm. It is enough to cock an ear to the discourse of the times. Simple arguments, simpler phrases, sentimentalism, patriotic verbiage, ingratiating references to sport and pop – increasingly these are the stock-in-trade of most politicians, and not just on the Left; Conservatives are hard at work learning the language and stratagems of populism to compete with their opponents, to whom such techniques, historically, have come more naturally.

So what is new? Has not our adversarial system always encouraged demagogy? It certainly has. Yet recently something fundamental has changed. When the parties had distinct ideologies their opposition was based somewhat more on principle. Now that party-political competition resembles a war between rival supermarkets, in which each seeks to out-sell the other by offering indistinguishable products at more advantageous prices, politics are becoming a populist charade played out by political elites. Whoever is in power is represented by their opponents as the bloodless executants of arrogant and unfeeling authority who are failing to implement the people's will.

The media, like politics, is a leading member of our populist oligarchy. Which means that it too must present itself as the opposite of what it is – an elite force in society whose power and authority have grown to the point where they rival, rather than counterbalance, those of government. Instead, TV and press magnificos project themselves as intrepid spirits taking the side of the little man against overbearing hierarchies, or as liberating society from its constraints and inhibitions. From time to time they can live up to the prospectus, by uncovering instances of political corruption or encouraging more enlightened sexual attitudes where they are needed. Essentially, however, the media – itself the most powerful and overbearing hierarchy of our time – is acting out the same anti-elite charade as that played by politicians.

By any objective measure Britain is neither a seriously corrupt nor a severely repressed society. Nor – residual problems of freedom of information aside – is the media subject to official censorship to any meaningful degree. It takes an inflamed imagination to see the media as a thorn in the side of the Establishment, when both press and television work happily (and profitably) within the established, neo-liberal commercial order. Their politics may vary from one organ to another but in essence their aims are near-identical: to maximize profits by exploiting their freedom to push their interpretation of news values or of sexual liberty to sensationalist or prurient limits – all, of course, in the people's name.

Education elites offer a further example of a simulated conflict with authority. Again we see one of the most deeply entrenched power-holders in society assuming a beleaguered posture – in this case a vow to protect children against heretical, anti-egalitarian values. In truth, teachers and educationists are no longer combating 'elitist' attitudes and practices in our schools, which in the state sector have all but vanished. That war was won long ago: that is why there are a mere 161 selective schools left outside the private sector. Those who oversee a system where some 90 per cent of pupils have little choice but to attend a single type of school are not anti-elitists, they are the elite. It is they who have the numbers and the power. It is they, and not Winchester or Eton College, who do most to set the tone in society. And like all elites they are intent on defending the reigning orthodoxy and on extending their power: hence their intolerance of the idea that a tiny percentage of selective schools should remain outside their hands. And whenever their quasi-monopoly of teaching philosophies is in any degree threatened, educational elites react forcefully to protect the *status quo*, usually by denouncing reforms as elitist.

In the arts a parallel process of inversion has long been underway. Here too those in authority (ministers, cultural officials and many an artist or performer) present themselves as anti-elitists whose leitmotiv is 'art for the many, not just the few'. There can be nothing wrong with that. As a slogan it is on a level with 'peace in our time' or 'work and bread for all': the sentiment is impeccable so long as one leaves aside the durability of the peace or the nutritious quality of the bread. As all power is vested (nominally) in the people, culture is transformed, Fourier-style, into anti-culture: a warm and friendly thing of which no one need feel in awe. Instead of being demanding, it becomes (in official mouths at least) an activity for which no specialist knowledge or discriminatory faculty is required.

When, shortly after coming to office, Chris Smith said that 'Cultural activity is not some elitist exercise that takes place in reverential temples aimed at the predilections of the *cognoscenti*', it was a defining moment in the rise of the new elites in culture, as well as a melancholy one for the English language. There was no need for Smith to say this. Just as it was open to Tony Blair to assert his determination to bring about social justice without claiming, absurdly and disingenuously, to be one of the rest of us, Smith could have restricted himself to vowing to improve access to the arts. But that was not enough. Then and since he has thought it necessary to attack 'cultural elites', in this instance somewhat carelessly defined as *cognos-*

centi, i.e. people who know what they are talking about. Never before has a minister of culture used knowledge as a pejorative term.

His excess of zeal in the populist cause is, in a sense, natural. The son of middle-class parents, who was educated at a highly selective school, studied at Cambridge and Harvard, and who is himself a *cognoscento* of Wordsworth, on whom he wrote a doctorate, has a lot to live down. Like a schoolchild over-anxious to insinuate himself into the favours of the biggest boys in the playground, Smith is liable to come under attack from those he tries most desperately to befriend. It could almost have been with the minister in mind that Tony Parsons, an (otherwise) intelligent and persuasive pop critic, wrote in the *Independent*: 'I consider myself part of the modern working class. We can go anywhere, do anything, earn a six-figure salary and do it all without changing our accents. I am happy to say that I haven't got a middle-class bone in my body. All the dreary tastes of the middle-classes . . . are anathema to me.' The spectacle of the middle-class Labour minister and the working-class boy made good engaged in a Dutch auction for the favours of what both mistakenly see as the masses, one sneering at expert knowledge, the other at those of non-proletarian birth, is an English classic.

Parsons's statement of beliefs is emblematic. Assertions of class superiority coupled with boasts about six-figure salaries are characteristic of inverted elites in popular culture. The combination of sanctimoniousness and ostentatious wealth is reminiscent of the *nouveau riche* industrial bourgeoisie at their most triumphant. Morally and financially Parsons leaves us in no doubt as to who, in the culture of a mass society, is top dog. Access to this exclusive caste, as to the aristocracy, turns out to be hereditary, a matter of blood and bones. Which leaves our minister of culture in the posture of a perpetual supplicant, who can never aspire to full admittance. The more obsequious he becomes towards them, the more the blue-bloods of pop, like the most fastidious of nobs, wince at his pretensions. That is what we saw in the Cool Britannia fiasco. And most humiliating of all, as a mere cabinet minister, Smith does not even earn a six-figure salary.

Amongst our populist oligarchs, business elites deserve special mention. They are important in their own right and because their activities impinge so closely on the oligarchy's other members, notably in culture and the media. Business is about permanent adaptation and the modern-minded man of commerce has not stood still where relations with the masses are concerned. He too has developed his ultra-democratic patter, to the effect that his prime concern in all he does is to maximize freedom of choice, the democracy of the markets. Again the rhetoric is the inverse of the reality. In truth, he is primarily concerned with eliminating competition and maximizing profits. Why else would he be in business? And if mass production and mass tastes should miraculously coincide, the vulgarity and uniformity that can result are no responsibility of his: the people have spoken and their word is law. So it is that homogenizing tendencies can be justified as being the result of individual choice and monopolistic designs are disguised by invocations of the gods of competition.

In an upside-down world where government portrays itself as anti-government and culture as anti-culture, business too must take care to project an anti-business image. 'Commerce' has disagreeable overtones of self-seeking, which in an egalitarian, Fourier-type order must be soothed away. The result is that the more narrowly profit-driven our leading commercial enterprises become, the more they seek to avoid any suggestion that they exist to make money. Instead PR folk sell their companies to the public as disinterested organizations of the charitable type. Their purpose is to create jobs, make their customers happy by providing them with lifestyles they would not otherwise enjoy, educate them about their products or entertain them with witty ads. That is when they are not preserving the environment or dedicating themselves to other philanthropic pursuits. These include scientific research, rectifying the imbalance in trade, fostering goodwill between nations by investing in foreign countries or bringing culture to the masses through sponsorship of the arts. Any anti-business worth the name will have installed what Tom Wolfe called its 'turd on the plaza' outside its company HQ, in the form of a sculpture or other art object, as a contribution to urban aesthetics and an earnest of its selfless devotion to the Muses.

Clarity about the relations between culture and commerce is essential to an understanding of the workings of an ultrademocracy. It also helps to dispel any lingering illusions that the new elites are confined to the egalitarian Left. Despite mounting evidence to the contrary, we persist in seeing modern business and left-of-centre politics as opposing forces, and to pit the noble ideals of The People against the greed and rapacity of commerce. (The myth is all the more strange since the majority of people, in one form or another, are engaged in commerce, not least when they buy and sell their flats or houses, sometimes at an enormous, unearned, untaxed profit.) One of the most striking aspects of our modern mass society is the growing affinities between the aims and methods of big business and those of egalitarian elites. Far from being condemned to eternal opposition, in highly commercialized populist democracies the two become brothers under the skin. The saying that the Right have won in economics and the Left in culture is one of the more convincing clichés of the times, yet it overlooks the most important consequence of their respective triumphs: that the victors have done a deal. It is enough to chart the points of convergence between business and the modern Left to understand the reasons for their tacit accommodation. Commerce and the Left share a revulsion to anything smacking of exclusivity: business because its dreams are of expansion, and excluding customers is not what it is about; egalitarians for obvious reasons. In pursuing their separate strategies, each has its eye on the big numbers: egalitarians are happy with a mass culture, business seeks mass markets, and each strives endlessly towards the populist norm. That is why TV advertisements and party political broadcasts are increasingly interchangeable, stock characters and all. For their differing reasons each sees the needs and desires of mass man as sacrosanct: for the egalitarian he is an ideological client, for the businessman he is a paying customer.

Where their interests appear to clash, often we find a disguised convergence. Schools are the best example. Educationists complain about pressures from the business world for more vocational courses and sigh at the neglect of the higher purposes of education. At the same time they are suspicious of any over-emphasis on the past, preferring what they see as 'relevant' studies, including the use of commercial culture (TV series, rock songs in music lessons, popular fiction) as teaching materials. In practice, therefore, the advocates of the higher purposes of education frequently go along with low expectations, necessary to promote 'access' and equality. The result is an unofficial division of labour between commerce and education. The tastes and values inculcated in schools reflect the fads and fashions of the times, while business waits at the gates to pocket the profits. An egalitarian educational culture delivers consumers to business like heifers to the abattoir, except that even heifers can put up a bit of a struggle when they see what's coming to them.

In both commerce and education the guiding norms are quantitative: the educationist watches the number of pupils who have passed an examination or gained a degree mount from year to year with the same benevolent eye as investors in downmarket TV when they survey their surging ratings. High levels of a literary or artistic culture are no more a priority for commerce than for educators bent on a massifying agenda. Of course, there are schools and teachers, not only in the private sector, who understand exactly what is happening and aspire higher. But the pressures of an anti-elite oligarchy in commerce and culture are relentless and confront them with a near impossible task.

Schools do not only manufacture the workforce, they manufacture consumers, and the philosophy of contemporary education could scarcely be better geared to producing the right kind of consumer from the business point of view. The educationist would, of course, refute this, insisting that teaching methods geared to social realities and annual rises in examination passes can be compatible with high standards. In scrupulous hands, this indeed can be the case, though inevitably such denials remind us of the businessman who objects to the accusation that he is engaged in the mass production of cheap, meretricious goods. True, the man of commerce believes in competition. Yet in the cultural sphere – TV, the press, the arts – the biggest money is to be made in competing downwards. That is why the anti-competitiveness preferred by many teachers can be reconciled with competitive market pressures. One by-product of anti-elitism in education is restricted vocabularies, and one has only to listen to the average commercial radio show to discover how the cheery, monosyllabic chat of the callers and presenters blends seamlessly with the cheery, monosyllabic ads.

The commerce of feeling also brings together schools and the market. For the mass marketeer, as for the cultural egalitarian, feelings are supreme, simply because we all have them. Intellect, being less equally distributed, is seen as divisive, a non-profitable product. The classroom instils sentimentalism, the media and the entertainment industry sell sensation. Schools encourage children to trust their instincts; business insists that the customer is always right. 'Feeling comfortable with yourself' is a supreme value in the schoolroom and exploited in the ads ('Go out and treat yourself! You know you deserve it!') Doctrines of self-restraint are anathema: to the businessman they impede the development and sale of new products, to the egalitarian they hark back to classical and therefore 'elitist' values.

The British tabloid press is an example of what commerce and an ultra-democratic educational culture can achieve in harness. Rupert Murdoch, in common with many a teacher, is an avowed anti-elitist. It is a nice irony that the tighter the grip of populists in the media on our newspapers or television, the louder the complaints from the populists who preside over much of our education. Murdoch papers criticize the teachers for being left-wing, and teachers are critical of the 'dumbing down' right-wing press. Who in their right mind, they lament, would buy a Murdoch product? Where could the consumers have learned such lowly tastes? For all their mutual antipathy, Murdoch and the teachers are what Marxists used to call objective allies.

The narrowing gap between commerce and culture brings politicians of the Left and Right ever closer together. As ultra-democracy takes hold, both Labour and the Conservatives are in the process of bending their principles in the required direction. When the Left pour indiscriminate praise on popular culture they are lowering the horizons of those at the poorer end of the social scale, whose interests they profess to champion. And when they intrude the market ethos indiscriminately into the media, the arts and education, the Right forfeit their claims to be the upholders of 'traditional values'. What we are seeing is a squaring of the circle, as Right and Left converge hungrily on a populist agenda. In the past, socialists (Tawney, for example) and paternalist Tories would have had little compunction about enunciating standards from above. Now, in pursuit of equality, the Left insist on 'culture for the many, not just the few', with scant regard for the level of the culture in question. Meanwhile the Right, in pursuit of profit, invoke the slogan 'let the people choose'.

For all the adversarial bluster in Parliament, in the real world the two slogans blend into one: give the people what they want. For Left and Right the enemy – 'elitism' – is the same. New Labour denounces its cultural critics as diehard traditionalists. The Tories condemn those who question the dogma of competition in broadcasting or the arts as cultural snobs.

Whether the driving ideology is that of the free market or of the anti-elite Left is immaterial. The two creeds reinforce one another, with the results that we see.

Why does any of this matter? If we can see through their disguises, and they are hardly foolproof, and their hypocrisies are derided in the media, which happens, why concern ourselves overmuch with the game the new elites are playing? The reason is that the game is serious. Misconceptions about the nature and role of elites cast a pall over democracy. A healthy democracy would be one led by elites of talent or accomplishment, whether in business, sport, government or the arts, with access open to all. Responsibility goes with authority and high amongst the obligations of the 'elect' would be a duty to foster the aspirations of people less fortunate than themselves to emulate them and to join their number. In other words, there can be no elite worth the name that does not encourage the common man or woman to aspire to its condition (though we should remember that many people lead happy and valuable lives without aspiring to join elites of any kind). In the postwar period Britain edged further towards that ideal, through the lowering of class barriers, improvements in education, greater social justice and the prospect of a higher level of culture for all. The assumption was that progress would be linear. Populist democracies led by inverted elites put these gains at risk.

In an ultra-democracy mass man finds himself boxed in by champions and defenders. The newspaper editor defends his right to know but not to think. The educationist defends his right to learn – in moderation and in easy stages – and to think like everyone else. However gruesome or inane the spectacle, the TV producer defends his right to look, just as the businessman defends his customer's absolute liberty to choose – from the selection he chooses to make available and at the price the market chooses to name. The politician defends his right to accumulate rights and the scientist promises him pretty much anything, from cheap food to the child of his choice, all at nil cost to his ethics or to his environment. And the arts apparatchik chucks him under the chin and tells him not to worry his head about the acquisition of culture, since culture is what we say it is.

The new elites coddle and cajole mass man like a winsome child. Contemplating their behaviour – the politician's glabrous smile, the arts person oiling his way into the affections of the young, the smooth-tongued businessman promoting his mind-numbing products, the BBC executive promising both more accessibility and the maintenance of Reithian standards – one wonders at society's ability to recruit elites whose function it is to behave as courtesans of The People. But then the new elites are rarely men and women of distinction; indeed, the less distinguished they are the more fitted they will be for their task. Who better to exalt the mediocre than an elite of mediocrities?

It is said of slave-owning societies that the masters suffered alongside their victims, in the sense that the institution of slavery debased their moral lives. The same can be said of populist elites, who by their actions (or passivity) debase the society in which they and their children are destined to live. Though they frequently exist in a different social sphere (higher incomes, private or quasi-selective schools, middle-class enclaves, wider cultural interests) from those whose interests they purport to champion, the new elites can become victims of their own actions in two main ways.

The first is by fostering an underclass. The phenomenon is well advanced in America, where middle-class families are driven from city centres to suburbs like wandering tribes, or fortify themselves in upmarket ghettos, to escape the social breakdown and cultural impoverishment that, directly or indirectly, they may have had a hand in bringing about. Low-achieving education policies, a vulgarized media or relaxed attitudes to family disintegration or drugs make for gratifying anti-authoritarian stances, but they do not make for cosy neighbours.

The second way in which the 'masters' can suffer alongside the 'slaves' is when they or their families become infected by the populist values they promote for profit or position. By a process of indolence, contamination or self-indulgence, counterfeit vulgarians can find themselves metamorphosing into the genuine article. Cultures are contagious things, not least the populist variety, which is sweet to the tongue and easy on the mind, and before they know it affectation has crossed into authenticity, and the new elites begin playing out their demotic mime with Stanislavskian sincerity. In public they strike demonstratively open-minded attitudes on what constitutes art, or in favour of the ultra-liberalization of social mores, only to find that in private life it becomes hard to stop the act. By dint of pandering to mass taste the new elites can become mass men and women themselves, in the unflattering sense of the term.

The arts or media person begins by defending the genuinely original and truly exciting against disapproving conservatism, then feels bound to smile indulgently on the latest fad and ends with indiscriminate approbation for whatever is new. Their indulgence is no longer simulated: their critical faculties blurred by an anxiety to please and by praise for their receptivity to novelty, they have actually grown to like it, irrespective of what 'it' may be. In similar fashion, the English graduate turned politician, journalist, advertising executive or TV producer gives up reading anything more demanding than the current best-seller. The ebbs and flows of fashion will henceforth dictate how they spend their lives, just as they do the lives of others. Their literary education has ceased to be a stage in their personal development and become a mere stepping stone to 'a career in the masses', whose tastes they find themselves first mimicking, then absorbing. They may have begun with loftier expectations, but their experience has cured them of that, and their ambitions for themselves have declined in line with their ambitions for society.

Populist affectations can rub off on the children of the new elites, sometimes to their disquiet. The defenders of new methods in education, perturbed by the standards of their local schools, exercise their middle-class prerogative to decamp to you know where – while continuing to defend the new methods. Examples amongst politicians are too flagrant to mention; amongst media and arts elites there are many, many more. Similarly the middle-aged columnist who calls for the liberalization of drugs, with less thought for the pros and cons than for the plaudits of the young, discovers that his son or daughter is on the road to addiction; if they were legalized, who knows, the road could be shortened. Then there is the determinedly anti-elitist don who watches in mild dismay as the cultural proletarianism he has espoused for the benefit of his students is embraced by his young family. This was not what he meant at all; his demotic *singerie* was directed at other people's children, not his own.

Previous elites went to great trouble to instil into their children the values of their caste. Anti-elite elites, not surprisingly, can be in some confusion as to what those values are. The result can be seen in a tendency amongst the children of new elite parents to become culturally *déclassés*. I do not mean that they have opened their minds to popular culture; I mean that popular culture may be all there is in their minds. Not that this will prevent them succeeding in their chosen careers; rather the opposite, and since nepotism is rife amongst the new elites they can count on a hand up from their parents, or simply by their name. The press and TV are full of examples of this baleful new form of dynastic influence.

Meanwhile genuine elites of talent and intelligence will be marginalized. Even if invited to simplify their messages for mass consumption, they may decline to join the game. Those who hold to their values will shy away from public exposure or retire into isolation and become in reality what they are accused of being – divorced from the people. Already there is a striking absence in the media of the voices of those scientists, writers, artists, philosophers or thinkers who refuse to take the populist whip. The result over time seems likely to be a decline in public life, as ever more spheres of society become dominated by a sham elite, whose final effrontery is to deny that it exists.

4

The Fine English Art of Condescension

> The French way of thinking is that they do not wish to have superiors. The English wish to have inferiors. The Frenchman constantly raises his eyes above himself in anxiety. The Englishman lowers them beneath him in satisfaction.
>
> Tocqueville, *Voyage en Angleterre*

One reason egalitarian elites seem likely to flourish are the attractions, peculiarly strong in our case, of a patronizing posture. For reasons it might be damaging to the prestige of the race to probe, the English excel all rivals in the art of condescension. It is a failing with export potential: American commentators have noted that, when seeking editors to popularize (i.e. dumb down) a newspaper or magazine, the publishers frequently hire British personnel. Since America has a superabundance of home-grown populists this seems like a case of coals to Newcastle. The explanation can only be that the quality of the coal – i.e. the condescension – is superior to the local product.

We speak of the free-born Englishman, yet equality for us often appears to be an affectation, not in the blood. We hand it down like a gift from on high for which the populace should be grateful, even though its *de haut en bas* origins negate its purpose. There can be no equality that is dangled over people like an apple on a string, to be jerked away at will by whoever does the dangling. Nor can genuine equality be tossed to the masses with gracious gestures. There are arguments for and against egalitarianism in culture, depending on the sense in which the word is used and the level to which the equalizers aspire. But in a society where equality is as strained as mercy, such a culture will always be a self-conscious, unnatural thing. As we are seeing in New Labour's attitudes to the arts, and most glaringly in the Dome, what matters is not that the masses should look up in aspiration: it is that the elites should be able to lower their eyes beneath them in satisfaction.

An Englishman indulging in a bout of condescension, like an Englishman undergoing a fit of morality, presents a striking spectacle. Specimens can be seen on television. Watching the condescender extol to the skies a popular new film, middle-brow novel or fashionable rock band can be a disturbing experience; there may be nothing much wrong with the film, the novel or the band, but there is quite definitely something wrong with him. More concerned with his own generosity than with the recipient of his praise, he will tend to overflow. Though a man of broad culture, he can never be heard enthusing over a play or classical concert or literary novel in quite this way. And though generally of an undemonstrative disposition, suddenly the condescender is all violent gesticulations and verbal excess.

He does not say he rather enjoyed the book or the band, he says he adored it. It is never just good, it is brilliant, sometimes out of this world. As the spasms of onanistic delight work towards a convulsion, the eyes close and the vowels in words like 'amazing' and 'fantastic' are elongated, partly to fill time while the condescender gropes for further superlatives. There being none to be had, his head jerks from side to side in an ecstasy of frustration before he simmers down, often with the dying protestation, 'No, really!' As if we could doubt his sincerity.

Condescension affords the Englishman an almost sensual pleasure. It is one of the few to which he feels able to give himself wholeheartedly, so he goes at it with a will. If, for purposes of anthropological study, he were to be photographed at the highpoint of his ecstasy, the clinched eyes and pained expression would appear to suggest extremes of suffering and, trite as they are, psycho-sexual explanations are unavoidable. For at the climax of his act of condescension he is frequently experiencing something that is at once sensuous and divine: a mystic union with the masses.

It is not for nothing that nuances of the verb 'to condescend' occupy an entire page in the *Oxford English Dictionary* (full edition) and that no less than twenty-nine examples are given. Anyone thinking of making his or her career in the masses would do well to study its etymology. Words accrete flavours, and it can be enlightening to match current practice to historical meanings:

TO CONDESCEND

1. *To sink willingly to equal terms with inferiors.* This basic meaning of the word is increasingly traduced in highly revealing ways. When journalists or critics attack a performance or a broadcast for being condescending, often they do not mean that it has been presented in a way that insults the intelligence of the audience by 'sinking to equal terms with inferiors'. They mean the opposite: that the insult consists in doing things that risk going over the head of the man or woman in the street. In this way the meaning of the word is gradually inverted. Those who water down an opera or an exhibition to court public favour escape censure, while those who remain true to their values and seek to raise the level of appreciation of others are deemed guilty of condescension. To pepper a political speech with Latin tags, or insist that young children watch a classical play in Greek, may be wildly optimistic, pompous or plain stupid. The one thing it is not is condescending. The point is important as an example of how language, like egalitarian elites, ends up on its head, in such a way that the wrong person is charged with the wrong offence.

2. *To make concessions.* This evokes a picture of those in authority engaging in a perpetual negotiation with those beneath them. It is clear who tends to make the most concessions. For example, schoolteachers who listen in orgasms of enthusiasm to their pupils' banal accounts of what they have seen on TV. Or jacket-less politicians in a roomful of suits. Or the fracturing of politicians' language into monosyllables, this being all people are deemed capable of swallowing at a go, the above-mentioned orgasmic teachers having failed to instil in them in youth any knowledge of or affection for the richer variations of the English tongue.

3. *To comply.* This is close to 'to make concessions', though in this case the implication is that the concessions have been made under duress. This meaning induces a more sympathetic attitude towards inverted elites, reminding us that not all of them have willingly stood on their heads; they may simply be complying with market forces. A choice instance was the reluctant decision by the Oxford University Press to abandon their modern poetry publishing in order to comply with a decision by the public, less reluctantly reached, to exercise their inalienable democratic right not to read it.

4. *To defer.* An intriguing meaning, which would appear to go against the very essence of the word 'to condescend'. This suggests a motion from the top down, whereas 'to defer' suggests the opposite: to recognize superiors. A moment's thought reveals that these meanings are not as contradictory as they seem: it is *because* they have a healthy regard for the power of men and women in the mass that the new elites defer to them. Deferring to someone from a superior position involves great agility, but affords twice the pleasure and occasionally an illicit thrill. An example would be the somewhat exquisite don who assures you he is absolutely passionate about gangsta rap (he may indeed be, but with the English, you never know).

5. *To conspire.* In condescending to populist opinion the new elites conspire with the masses, and vice versa, to lower

expectations in social or cultural life. Media moguls, for example, are criticized for debasing the standards of our press and TV. So they often do, but they are working hand in glove with their customers. The English complain that there is nothing in the press or TV worth reading or watching, while buying more newspapers and watching more TV than anyone in Europe.

6. *To patronize.* This meaning of 'to condescend' brings us back to base. In 'sinking willingly to equal terms with inferiors' egalitarian elites are not demonstrating their solicitude for the common man: they are showing who are the inferiors and who is the *patron.* Their attitude is reminiscent of the figure of the donor in early Northern Renaissance painting. Normally he is a reverential-looking fellow on his knees, praying, though his posture of submission should not be misunderstood. He is the artist's patron, who has paid a large sum to buy his place in the picture, so as to demonstrate his piety and as an insurance policy with Higher Authority. When our anti-elite elites prostrate themselves before the public their humility is as genuine as his, and their aims are not dissimilar: to ingratiate themselves with our contemporary Lord and Master, the masses, while ensuring that they feature as prominently as possible in the foreground of the picture.

Like some infinite sequence encoded in the national genes, the combinations and recombinations of condescension are inexhaustible. It is commonly thought to be a disease of the upper classes, yet variations are to be found throughout society. 'We must be thoroughly democratic', says a character in Bernard Shaw's *John Bull's Other Island,* 'and patronize everyone without distinction of class.' And that is what we do. So refined is the practice that we can condescend upwards as well as downwards, and from any social position: the top, the middle or the bottom. There are not too many countries where it is possible for almost everyone to patronize almost everyone else, yet somehow we manage it. In Britain the purpose of striving higher in society is not simply to reach a superior level of income, status or culture: it is to look down from an ever greater height. Once the attraction of looking down might have consisted in a pleasurable distaste for the hoi polloi – 'Thank God I am not as other men are.' Nowadays the pleasure is more likely to come from a show of magnanimity towards them. The difference, in practice, can be slight. Meanwhile, as we shall see, those in the middle or close to the bottom find ingenious ways to condescend to those at the top.

Socially speaking, our condescenders fall into three main types.

1. *The Lordly and Munificent*. This form of condescension goes with elevated status, say the upper middle classes and above. Its main ingredients are a demonstrative broad-mindedness, a patrician indulgence and a flamboyant liberalism, frequently spiced with a dash of quirkiness. Sometimes the breadth of mind can be genuine. More often it is designed to point up the difference between aristocratic *désinvolture* and narrow, judgemental middle-classes attitudes. The flamboyantly liberal stances are a reminder that the upper classes are above morality. The indulgence to inferiors is calculated to draw the notional response: 'You're a gent, Sir.'

Quirkiness can be a useful addition to the mix. It by no means necessarily reflects recondite tastes or an original cast of mind. On the contrary, quirkiness, like originality, is frequently a substitute for intelligence: the sign of an empty or conven-tional mind in search of easy distinction. A willed 'originality' is the simplest way of setting oneself above the herd and of keeping others on the hop. They can never be sure what you are going to say or do next, and so are reduced to a position of inferiority.

'What do you think of Tony Blair?'

'I don't mind his policies, it's his frightful taste in socks (ties, suits, shoes, braces, women) I can't stand.'

Or: 'I see those dreadful football fans have been rioting in Europe again.'

'Why shouldn't they? Shows spirit, and reminds Johnny foreigner who's boss.'

Quirky responses have the attraction of dispensing the condescender from thinking about the issue or, assuming he or she has a view, from showing their hand (the preservation of mystique) or expressing a strong opinion (vulgar by definition). The technique is most often used by would-be, rather than genuine aristocrats. The latter might easily be feeble- or lazy-minded enough to resort to it, but would be under less compulsion than *arrivistes* or social mountaineers to emphasize the distance between themselves and others. It is a sad truth that the trick of being quirky or 'original' normally works, appealing as it does to the more servile streak in our national make-up.

2. *The Anxious Middle.* A more numerous and complex category of condescender, this consists of people in the middling range of professions (journalists, computer analysts, civil servants) who are permanently unsure of what they should be thinking. Their greatest terror (and they are a fearful lot) is of finding themselves classified with the old, the conservative, the unstylish, the unprogressive. Once the males of the species could be readily identified by their abnormally adventurous ties; now they attempt to achieve the same effect by wearing no tie at all, which is a relief for everyone. There is a touch of desperation as they ponder, on any given question, which way to jump – a nerviness that can frequently be observed in their eyes or in other body language. Their intermediate position in society sometimes requires them to condescend in two directions at once. For example, their opinion of The Lordly and Munificent condescender might be: 'Of course he's a total fraud, but you have to admit he's terribly amusing', or 'Did you see that thing he wrote? It's really not bad, given that he's an idiot.'

Culturally The Anxious Middle are in a mess. What, for

example, are they to make of Proust? Unlike The Lordly and Munificent, they cannot make a virtue of saying that they have never read him and never intend to. In the upper classes and above that would be a point of distinction; in The Anxious Middle it would be mere ignorance and proof that they had had an indifferent (even state) education. So they are driven to adopt a variety of stratagems, involving both upwards condescension ('I tried reading him, but I never got beyond the first volume. He's quite a good writer but frankly I don't understand what the song and dance is about') and down ('Joanna Trollope is the Proust of our time.')

Politically, The Anxious Middle are unstable, vacillating from Left to Right and back, roughly in time with the cost of their dangerously ambitious mortgage. Replete with insecurities, they are crucified on the up/down Left/Right cross. Which way are they to incline, in a given situation? How will the image they covet – as stylish, modern-minded, somewhat radically inclined folk (NB the absence of tie) – be affected? Their secret dream is to be in the position of The Lordly and Munificent, to smile down on their fellows, throw off some inane observation and be thought amusing. As it is, The Anxious Middle do not have that much to look down on and are too anxious to smile much. In their heart of hearts they would love to pull the 'quirky and original' trick, but are not sure they can carry it off.

The Anxious Middle are forever casting round for people to patronize, or with whom they can ingratiate themselves. It might be the upper classes one day, the proletariat the next. The Lordly and Munificent are praised as 'wags' or 'free spirits', while the genuine or would-be proletarians (pop types, football fans) are lauded for their youthful zest (the Anxious Middle were born middle-aged) and somewhat frightening energy. If in the end they come down on the side of populism it is through a mixture of indolence and calculation: things appear to be going the populists' way, there are a lot of them and it seems wise to keep in with them.

One way and another The Anxious Middle have a poor time of it. Their position is a vexing one, frequently revealed in an expression of fretful non-commitment, puzzlement and some sadness. Their problem is insoluble, because it springs from their consciousness of their unstable status in society, which turns their lives into a permanent identity crisis. If only they knew who they were, The Anxious Middle would love nothing more than to be themselves.

3. *The Condescender de Bas en Bas.* The fact that this type can exist at all is an example of the English social genius. Normally he or she is a person of lower-middle-class origins (a teacher, council employee, a leftist MP). They praise working-class styles of life partly because resentment at the depth of their own mediocrity drives them to seek out others to patronize, and the proletariat, such as it remains, is all there is. The type can be called The Condescender *de Bas en Bas* because he is the only one who plays down to people on an intellectual and cultural level not far removed from his own. Another reason to patronize the proletariat is fear that the smarter amongst them may be smarter than himself.

The *de Bas en Bas* type despises both The Lordly and Munificent and The Anxious Middle for being part-time condescenders to the lower orders, whose hearts are not in it. Culturally, he is drawn to the pseudo-revolutionary and self-consciously anarchic (druggie novelists – more Prousts of our time – excremental modern art). To feel the full stinging lash of his populist snobbery, and see his lip curl in superb disdain, it is enough to get the name of a pop band wrong, to be ignorant of a football score or not to have seen a film. Yet he has a fey side to him and his private tastes and personal behaviour can be endearing. The man who thinks society should be wrenched up by the roots like a mouldy cabbage can be found peaceably immersed in a Terry Pratchett or *The Lord of the Rings*, while supervising his children at play in the park.

His politics are a snarl of disapproval of all parties as being in it together. If Britain had ever had a serious communist party the *de Bas en Bas* Condescender would have voted for it. But Marxism can be a horribly disciplined business, and because of the mushy thinking, sentimentalism and essential harmlessness of people like himself, it never has.

It is impossible to discuss condescension without a word on Princess Diana. I hesitate to add to the gross national product on her life and death, yet in the cause of advancing the argument it must be done. Our late Princess symbolized more powerfully than anything else the shift from the old elites to the new. Diana was the *fine fleur* of British condescension, a study in herself of the art of making a career in the masses, a one-woman distillation of the aims and methods of inverted elites. This was no mere wheedling politico or opportunist editor or calculating businessman, but a princess, in whom the art of patronage and manipulation from on high appeared instinctive, in the blood. It is hardly surprising that populist oligarchs in politics and the media warmed to her as they did. In life, Diana was their role model, in death, their patron saint.

Diana was a member of the Royal Family, the most traditional and wealthy elite in the land. Her attitudes and instincts were conservative and patrician, particularly when it came to conserving for herself the rights, riches and privileges of her caste. Her plangently humanitarian attitudes were no doubt to an extent genuine. But she was no naïve philanthropist, showing no disposition to distribute her worldly goods, of which she appeared inordinately fond, to the British or Third World poor. Nor was she in any sense a social revolutionary, a sort of female Philippe Egalité, who at least had the consistency to support the abolition of the monarchy. ('Elites in a stage of decline', wrote Pareto, 'generally display humanitarian sentiments and great kindness; but this kindness, provided it is not simply weakness, is more seeming than real.')

Her preferred companions were celebrities, the media, film

people, fashion folk, tycoons – the frothier side of the new elites – and her 'revolt' against the old elite of which she was a part was confined to opposing its constraints on her personal freedom, and its traditionalist behaviour. She did not object to the monarchy, she objected to its style. What she wanted was status and popularity – the dual position aspired to by all inverted elites. In her case this meant being seen simultaneously as a Royal and a commoner, a champion of the people and a celebrity, a member of the elite and of the mass.

In one sense she was well suited to this latter role. Her facial beauty apart, she was an undistinguished woman – a mass woman, in fact. Diana was common in the etymological meaning of the word, which is to say that her characteristics are those commonly found in a certain type of attractive woman at all levels of society. She was wilful, self-centred, self-indulgent, under-educated and of no more than average intelligence (though with the instinctive cleverness of cunning), manipulative and prone to use her looks to get her way. Her philanthropic instincts, though worthy enough, were common as well, in the sense that most of us are reasonably humane people, who would be inclined to even greater acts of humanity if we had an income of several million a year and were princes or princesses.

Her commonness was not reprehensible and there is no reason we should expect royalty to be better men or women than ourselves. Monarchists have unanswerable arguments on the theme. If Diana had shown more positive traits than she did, such as high intelligence, dignity, self-restraint, devotion to duty or pretty well any other human virtue, it would have been intimated that such qualities were proof, should it be needed, that royalty are a superior breed. When royal persons commit adultery, jib at their duties, consort with shady millionaires or indulge themselves in any way, the same monarchists will pronounce themselves shocked at our shock: the whole point of royalty, they will then argue, is their ultimate humanity and ability to represent the common man or woman with all their faults. So it is that a strong character in royalty incarnates the strengths of the people, while a weak one reflects the people's fallibility. Such is the dead-end argument only fools or constitutionalists will join. What matters here is the convenience of the 'Royals are only human' argument as it relates to elites. What it comes down to is that, at Diana's level, inverted elites must be allowed inverted norms of conduct, in the same way that great artists, geniuses or celebrities are seen as people to whom conventional modes of behaviour do not apply. The artists redeem themselves by the brilliance of their works, the geniuses by their genius, the celebrities by their celebrity, and Diana by her gift for communing with the people. Which is to say that being nice to the public exculpates you from accusations of bad behaviour, in the way that a wheedling child can get away with murder. And if royalty and celebrity are conjoined, as in Diana, and communing with the people becomes something of a profession, when it comes to the amount of human fallibility to be pardoned in the princess, the sky is the limit.

Thus the new elites free themselves from all constraints of duty, while preserving – or in Diana's case enhancing – their status in the public eye. A populist indulgence is deemed to have been granted to Diana by the objects of her condescension, the people – or rather by politicians, the media and the Church acting on their behalf. Little wonder they all saw Diana as a model of public relations. Film stars, over-sexed ministers, loose-living businessmen and the sinful clergy would give anything for such immunity from moral laws.

Populists are adept at ingratiating themselves with the 'victims' of society, but Diana did better. Long before anyone thought to call President Clinton's wife 'The First Victim', Diana conferred on herself the crown as Victim Number One. Without showing any readiness to sacrifice one iota of her wealth or position, she convinced the impressionable that to be a member of an elite was to suffer. We are all familiar with 'poor little rich

girl' films, which manage to persuade us for the requisite hour
and a half that the privileged too are deserving of our pity, and
that the amount of sympathy expended should be in proportion
to the wealth and status of the heroine. But with Diana there
was a difference. In the films the poor little rich girl pines to give
it all up to run away with her gypsy, destitute artist or honest
cobbler. Diana managed to have it all ways: somehow she
persuaded the public to pity her for being stuck in the richest
and most prestigious hierarchy in the land, and to pity her for
running away with the starstruck son of a billionaire.

Traditional elites, such as the monarchy, require only our
respect. Inverted elites are more demanding: as well as deferring
to their status, we must give them our hearts. (The anxiety of
new-style politicians such as Tony Blair to be liked for themselves is another example.) Diana played adroitly on the schizophrenic spirit of the age. It is one that pines for glamour to spice
the drabness of democracy, which is at once deferential and
self-assertive, tough-minded about money and soft in the head
about anything else.

The politics of the affair were revealing. Despite their different
agendas on royalty, Left and Right fell over each other to claim
her as their own. On the Left antagonistic stances to royalty
were cast aside like wooden swords at the end of a play. On the
Right, reservations about Diana as a cuckoo in the royal nest
were abandoned with the same alacrity, and the cuckoo transformed, miraculously, into a swan. Newspapers with High Tory
instincts, who had previously argued that the worst thing that
could happen to the monarchy would be its popularization,
sensed the popular mood and became overnight advocates of
change. As Burke almost said, a royal family that has no means
for its reform has no means to ensure its preservation. The
masses had spoken (or rather sobbed) and political reality must
be heeded. If the price of the salvation of the monarchy and of
the hierarchies of which it was the summit was populism, then
we are all populists now.

For a moment after her death it seemed that the barriers of Left and Right had melted in a hot profusion of tears – though behind the sodden hankies each was watching the other to see who would capture the lion's share of the inheritance: the affections of the people. Like football teams competing for a star player to boost the fortunes of their club, or tabloids bidding for lurid memoirs, politicians of all parties and their backers in the media threw themselves into battle to claim first rights to her ghost. The Tories saw Diana as more useful to them in death than in life, since cultivating her memory gave them a chance to keep the old elites going. For the Left, it was a chance to consolidate the position of the new. So it was that everyone, from leftist feminists to royalist pantaloons such as Norman St John Stevas, hurled themselves on her bier and claimed her as their own. Here was a perfect example of the humanitarian posturing among rival elites that Pareto had predicted.

When they said she was caring, they meant we are caring too. When they said she had feelings, they meant that, contrary to any impression we might have given, politicians are sentient beings. When they said she was against the Establishment, what they meant was, please do not mistake us for the new Establishment we most patently are. When they said she was a friend of the people and against the elite, they were disclaiming elite status. The parade of penitents in high places was a distasteful spectacle, not unlike a flagellant procession in medieval times.

Connoisseurs of the Diana phenomenon will have noted that its high-point came not at the funeral, but some months later. When Anthony O'Hear, a respected professor of philosophy, produced a critical analysis for inclusion in what was previously destined to be a somewhat obscure book, *Faking It*, his article was officially denounced, on the Prime Minister's personal orders, as the work of an out-of-touch right-wing snob. The fact that Blair was in Egypt at the time made it all the more remarkable that he should have felt the need to interrupt his diplomatic pursuits to quell this very minor eruption of anti-populist dissent at home. One is reminded of the official denunciations of dissident intellectuals in Eastern European countries under communism, or McCarthyism in the USA. For a strange moment one felt that, had it been in the Government's power to do so, Professor O'Hear would have been stripped of his citizenship and forcibly exported, like Solzhenitsyn, to any country that would be so unprincipled as to have him, or summoned to a specially constituted Star Chamber to face charges of un-British activities.

There can be different opinions about the proportion of the population that succumbed to Diana-latry (and according to some polls it was less than supposed), yet two things are beyond doubt. The first is that the powers that be – the Government, the opposition, the media, the Church, business – all worshipped at the shrine, castigating themselves as they wept, and solemnly pronouncing that we had become a better society as a result of her death. In a word, that she had died to save us all. The second incontrovertible fact is that the main victims of this officially condoned riot of emotion were less educated people at the lower end of the social pile. In Diana the conditions for a society based on the sentimentalizing of the masses and the perversion of genuinely democratic values were happily (or as I would argue, disastrously) conjoined. For those whose ambition it is to lord it over the masses, in modern times an essential precondition is to soften them up.

But the game of patronage needs two to play – the patronizer and the patronized – and the sad truth is that large swathes of the public at all social levels had responded swooningly to her insinuating style. To new elites with an interest in the infantilization of the people, the aftermath of the death of Diana was an object lesson in what could be achieved. Led by their populist notables, the British people behaved in a way it is painful to recall. Instead of calling the public to order, as any elite worthy of the name would have done, the Government, the media and business donned their cockards and urged them on in the biggest, the longest, the most abject and demeaning orgy of lachrymation the country has ever seen.

Most depressing of all was the strain of slavishness manifested in a supposedly free people: a reminder that ultra-democracies have little to do with the liberty and dignity of the individual. The new elites adopt a servile stance towards the people but insist on being repaid in the same coin. And the people – or enough of them to chill the heart – duly responded. Time after time, those who had met Diana and were interviewed in the media said the same thing: that the reason they cherished her memory was that, though they were just ordinary folk, the Princess had been nice to them. Often they added that she had behaved like an ordinary person herself. A more powerful tribute to the effectiveness of inverted elites, and their ability to exact deference by other means, is hard to imagine. One wanted to ask such people, 'What do you mean, you are "just an ordinary person"? Why shouldn't she be nice to you? And why should she not behave like the ordinary person she most patently was?'

In France or America it would be difficult to imagine the man or woman in the street who had shaken hands with their president dissolving into pools of awe over the fact that, ordinary though they were, the Great Man had treated them decently. They would have been proud to have met him because he was a symbol of their statehood and guarantor of their status as equal citizens. Their pride would be for themselves and for their democracy, and untinged with relief to have their commonness passed over with an indulgent smile. In Britain, a condescending touch never fails. If pop stars, prime ministers or princesses are nice to them, people respond with awe and gratification. In the free-born Briton a residue of subservience, it appears, lingers in the blood.

*

Devotees of Diana included people of both sexes and all social levels – men and women in the mass – yet there is no denying that women were most likely to fall victim to her patronage. As with education or the spreading of culture, the cause of feminism, when it falls into the hands of populist oligarchies, is instantly perverted. Egalitarian elites profess to be in the service of the new woman, yet the results of their devotion can be an intensified form of exploitation, in the guise of liberation. Here is a whole new category of customers for the merchants of condescension – rather more than half the population. And needless to say, some of the most active exploiters of the aspirations of women come from their own ranks.

It is scarcely necessary to list the offenders: editors of magazines who claim to be elevating the status of women even as they abase them to being objects of a voyeuristic culture; businesswomen selling 'empowering' accoutrements to fashion-crazed adolescents; female politicians or columnists who encourage the notion that the key to success in life is to be less rational and more emotive than the male. All are persuaded, and have succeeded in persuading others, that they have the welfare of their sex at heart. Which is strange, since the image of the ideal female they portray can be uncannily close to that of the least evolved male: thick-headed, hard-drinking, self-assertive, foul-mouthed and sexually incontinent.

Women, it is widely agreed, especially by women, have a somewhat different intelligence to men. From there to the assertion that emotion is a higher and truer form of sagacity is a big step – the equivalent of leading men to believe that brute force is the answer to every argument. Reading or listening to the views of the more light-minded women who tend to be selected as symbols of their sex in the media, one could be forgiven for suspecting that this is some kind of well-laid masculine plot. Women of all political persuasions can feel demeaned to find themselves represented in the public mind by purveyors of sentimental platitudes, or by air-headed col-

umnists who fluff or emote quirkily about nothing in particular.
The question arises, *cui bono*? Who selects these disgracers
of their sex, and with what purpose in mind? The reasons appear
to be populist in the commercial sense – the need to attract more
women listeners/viewers/readers, and the conviction that this is
best done by hiring lightweight in preference to bright women.
The same can clearly be true of males (e.g. laddish magazines),
yet one only has to think of the relative dearth of serious female
columnists and commentators in the press and on TV to become
aware of the imbalance. The new elites are feminists to a man.
But whereas social categories change, the profit motive doesn't,
there are millions of 'new women' to be played down to, business
is business and there are billions to be made. Diana, had she
lived, would have written a lovely column.

An alternative way of playing down to women is to play up to
them. When the representatives of womanhood thrust before us
are not sanctimonious sentimentalists, they tend to be Ama-
zonian tyros. It is hard to watch a TV film about business,
medicine, crime or the law without seeing companies led by
brilliantly mercantile women, hospitals staffed by female doctors or surgeons who combine humane feeling with good looks
and a steely competence, police stations dominated by women
detectives, tougher and more astute than any male, or a court-
room subjugated by female barristers, whose wigs are as devas-
tating as their interrogation techniques. Critics commend such
shows for their gritty realism.

We speak about 'role models' and 'positive images' as if they
were something new, yet they were and remain standard practice
amongst propagandists in totalitarian regimes. In communist
countries women were part of an idealized proletariat who in
films, plays and novels were invariably promoted to positions
of high responsibility: the factory manager, the Party secretary,
the military commander. Socialist realism required it, though
the truth was far less socialist and the reality stark. In everyday

life what tended to happen was that the proletariat got the positive images in the posters and plays while the elite of apparatchiks (overwhelmingly male) got the privileges and promotion. Not only was the *nomenklatura* almost exclusively masculine (remember that row of Homburgs when they lined up above Lenin's tomb), but frequently descended from bourgeois stock.

There is something to be learned here. With due allowance for the different forms of exploitation in socialist and capitalist societies, and for the fact that women in Britain are having a somewhat better time of it than the Russian proletariat, the analogy with the exploitation of women by our ultra-democratic *nomenklatura* becomes less fanciful than it seems. Communist parties too were committed, in formal terms, to gender equality, though like the upward march of the proletariat in the Soviet Union, the social promotion of women in Britain is often more apparent from the media than in reality. Meanwhile the aspirations to advancement of ordinary females can be crushed by condescension, smothered by praise.

Soviet workers, including women, were accorded every combination of virtues one could wish for: physical strength, a righteous concern for humankind and, those most enviable of gifts, a natural intelligence and extreme sincerity. Their bodies were those of gods, with chiselled features, commanding presences and perfect forms. And so it is – with a few human weaknesses thrown in for verisimilitude – with the idealized race of women projected by our new elites: the female surgeons, the barristers, the savvy, smart-talking, fearless crime-busters and the indomitable females in the pages of the press. Superwoman has superhuman powers of endurance (children and career), dominates male environments with ease (female powerhouses in the City) and cultivates physical strength (women working out). The most positive attribute ascribed to our poster-quality women is, of course, their emotional intelligence. This amalgam of the intellect and the feelings, an unbeatable combination, is a clear improvement on their proletarian counterparts in Russia, who for all their natural brains and extreme sincerity appeared a little wooden by comparison. But the killer quality of our superwomen as opposed to theirs is that, unlike the female proletariat in Soviet Russia or communist China, whose charms seemed hewn from stone, their capitalist counterparts are sexy too.

None of this is to say that these paragons of proletarian virtue or of Western superwomanhood can never be found outside the poster or the screen. I have come across examples of each – godlike Russian proletarians with open and noble faces and beautiful and brilliantly successful Western women (both of them, as it happens, often drunk). My point is the lack of typicality of the genre, and the advantages to the new elites of passing off the image for the reality. Idealization is a great way to do people down. They can never live up to the image you project of them, and the more you patronize them, like successful parents who gush over their children, the more you emphasize the gap between you and them. For all the heroic status foisted on her by the *nomenklatura*, the average Soviet woman had a poor time of it. When she was not shovelling ice on the streets, or queuing for the meanest necessities of life, she was being beaten insensible by a drunken husband.

Her British equivalent suffers a softer, though still unenviable fate at the hands of her idolaters and oppressors. Of course, there are many exceptions, especially at the better-off end of society, where genuinely liberated attitudes can be more prevalent. At more humble levels things have improved far less than we like to think. After a none too demanding schooling at the hands of egalitarian elites in education the average young woman will get a low-paid, low status job, spend her every last penny on beauty products thrust at her by commercial interests, pass her leisure hours mooning about pop stars and royalty and go to bed dreaming of being Geri Halliwell or Princess Diana. And it is quite possible that our idealized woman, encouraged to rely more on her emotions than her common sense, might make a less than ideal match, and end up being beaten insensible by a drunken husband.

5

A Culture of Pretence

It is one thing to lament, as Alan Bennett does, the English distaste for intellectuals, and quite another to think it amusing to call a play *Kafka's Dick*.

Lachlan Mackinnon in the *TLS*

To every fool is given his morsel of wisdom. When the former American Vice President Dan Quayle (of whom it was said 'He's cute, but can he type?') took to berating the 'Hollywood cultural elite' – meaning the liberal populists of the entertainment industry – for once he was on to something. The point at issue has been swallowed by time, yet the phrase 'the Hollywood cultural elite' remains suggestive. This being America, Quayle was attempting to speak in the name of the common man, who dislikes being looked down on by elites of any kind, whether they be of the liberal or traditional variety. In Britain we are a step behind the argument, and when you are a step behind Dan Quayle it is time to worry.

We have got it into our minds that cultural elites are invariably conservative, and persist in believing it even when it is clear from everyday reality that this has long ceased to be the case. The problem lies in our inability to distinguish between true and false egalitarianism. The British predicament is neatly illustrated by the success of *The Simpsons*, the American cartoon series which discriminating critics – amongst whom the author would naturally prefer to see himself – claim as a major cultural achievement of our times; certainly it is the major achievement of television. Like *Alice in Wonderland, Gulliver's Travels* or the works of Arthur Conan Doyle, its imaginative intelligence and technical brilliance are such that it would never occur to us to ask whether we are in the presence of high or popular art.

The Simpsons is about American small-town life, the life of the 'little man' if you like, be he or she shopkeeper, housewife, policeman, schoolmistress, bartender or that personification of the 'little man' at his most abject and heroic, Homer Simpson. Although there is an evil tycoon – Mr Burns, whose English accent is enough to betray his satanic inclinations – the show is not about honest folk who fall prey to corrupt elites. Honesty and corruption are widely distributed, in good egalitarian fashion, and none of the familiar antinomies are present. *The Simpsons* is not about class, northerners v. southerners, East v. West, rich v. poor, men v. women, blue v. white collar workers or blacks v. whites. To anyone but the cultural decoder it appears free of political or moral messages, certainly those the British are accustomed to hear. If it has been criticized on the American Right (by President Bush, amongst others) for showing the US to be a dysfunctional society, that is not because the show has any leftist message that I can discern; it can only be because humanity – American small town humanity or any other – tends to be dysfunctional.

The success of *The Simpsons* has not been achieved by playing to low taste, as American TV in its majority does. It enjoys a mass audience but the masses are not approached in a nervy, top–down spirit. That is why, as with *Alice in Wonderland*, everyone from children to intellectuals enjoys the show. And it is why it could never have been made in up/down Britain. You cannot look up to, or down on, Homer Simpson; he is just what there is. In contrast to the parochialism, self-consciousness and implicit moralizing of much British comedy, which leave you with a vaguely suffocated feeling, as anyone who has watched the show's best episodes knows, it exudes a sense of freedom.

A single joke in *The Simpsons* shows the depth of our malaise. In one episode a character named Otto disappears. When Bart Simpson, Homer's rapscallion son, asks what has happened to him, the reply comes: 'Forget Otto. That's one palindrome you won't have to worry about any more.' The gag is gone in a flash – the pace is fast – and the show reverts to inspired slapstick. That somewhat erudite one-liner in a programme watched by millions symbolizes the gulf between British and American attitudes to equality.

The makers of *The Simpsons* include graduates of elite American universities, and from time to time literary and historical allusions feature. (In another episode, a brief, surreal sequence has Homer's burping bar chums conversing, implausibly and to no purpose whatever, about Palmerston and Pitt the Younger; names not too many British viewers would recognize, let alone American. And the show's vocabulary is rich as well as rangy, with words like 'feculent' tossed in for the hell of it.) By including the 'palindrome' joke the scriptwriters and producers were merely being themselves. In all probability the gag was appreciated by a small percentage of the series' audience – a fact acknowledged in the spoof fanzine magazine the show's creators have published, where it is listed (though not explained) in the category of 'Things You May Have Missed'.

Try to imagine a similar crack featuring in a popular British cartoon. It is feasible, though unlikely. It is not that our scriptwriters would have lacked the wit to come up with the joke; in all probability the producers would have lacked the courage, or rather naturalness, to put it in. At some point in the editorial line someone would have blue-pencilled it on the grounds that it might be seen as yet another attempt by elites at the cultural exclusion of the masses. And the more elite the education he or she had enjoyed, the more heavily the gag would have been scored out. Literary jokes have social connotations and the lexicological innocence of the masses must not be sullied by fancy Graeco-Roman words. Dog-English obscenities yes, innuendo, constantly, since these are categories accessible to all. But a literary gag, thrown in for the delectation of 'the few rather than the many', absolutely not.

The truth is, of course, that it would be more patronizing to leave the gag out than to put it in. It is not snooty to introduce an audience to what for most people will be a new and recondite word; it is snooty to assume they are too bone-headed ever to understand it. The more fervent fans of the series may even have looked up 'palindrome' in the dictionary and learned what it meant. Their British equivalents would have continued in their ignorance, and their cultural vigilantes would have maintained their easy ascendency over them. Which in the last analysis is what it is all about. Still, we must hope for better times, and the fact that the British public seem to enjoy a show that does not patronize them is encouraging.

The crudity of the contemporary debate on whether our cultural life is 'dumbing down' or 'braining up' owes much to our atavistic political traditions. Again we are locked into up/down thinking, again we are called upon to march to the music of our Left/Right regimental bands. 'Anti-elitists' must give three huzzas for progress, 'elitists' must chant their war-cries against popular culture and insist that things are getting worse. There is no room for nuance, which is to say reality. Whatever their private misgivings, men and women of the liberal Left must make a show of perpetual optimism, even as they contemplate the brain-softening fare dispensed by much of the media, while conservatives must play out their role as cultural pessimists, even as they privately enjoy a raunchy TV show.

Clearly the picture is mixed: one only has to think of the fact that a good deal of intelligent, well-written journalism and criticism still makes it on to the pages of our press, of the high level of many of the popular books on science or of the excellence of some of our musical or theatrical performances, to realize that the Philistines are not everywhere in the ascendent. If forced to make a judgement, my own – as impressionistic as everyone else's – would be that our culture is moving in contradictory directions. Just as it is possible for the number of well-off people to grow while average earners remain static, and the poor get poorer in relative terms, so it is possible for the smart to get smarter and for the quantity of smart people to expand, while the numbers of the culturally destitute and the depth of their destitution increase too, again in relative terms. In other words, society could be braining up and dumbing down at the same time. If that is indeed what is happening it would be wholly compatible with the dominance in culture of anti-elite elites. For these are people whose primary interests, like those of elites in the past, revolve around themselves and their peers. The rest, as always, must take what they are given.

To engage the debate on culture on the anti-elitist's terms is always a mistake. Even such banal statements as 'some popular culture is impressive, much of it is puerile, and there is such a thing as higher cultural values' set the ultra-sensitive antennae of our ultra-democrats a-quiver. For them, to dismiss a particular style or genre of popular culture as rubbish, even when it palpably is, is to denigrate mass taste, and to talk of higher cultural values is to suggest that you have a down on lowly people. All this anguishing about social tone can encourage paralysis and stagnation, of the kind we are currently experiencing in our sitcoms or literary novels. Havering nervily between high and demotic forms, we end up with neither one thing nor the other: neither vitally popular art nor works that are in any sense lasting or profound. In most cases we are left with a sort of astutely pitched upper or lower middlebrow.

By contrast to the best American novels or TV scripts, whose cerebral highs and sassy lows are seamlessly intermixed, we are stilted, tongue-tied. The briefest comparison between British and American-made TV soaps and comedies highlights the problem. Ours tend to be formulaic affairs whose very titles are exercises in class-consciousness: *The Royle Family*, *Coronation*

Street, Dinner Ladies, EastEnders. This does not mean they cannot be amusing; it simply means that they are unlikely to tell us anything new about the world, or to rise above themselves. Watching them is like listening to the kind of House of Commons debate journalists invariably describe as 'lively' or 'vigorous': the experience can be momentarily stimulating, yet the sense of being cramped within a set of conventional attitudes, a sort of noisily mouldering tradition, is unrelenting. With their oratorical customs and tribal affiliations the MPs are playing their parts in a legislative sitcom and – like the stock TV characters – we have a fair idea what they are going to say before they speak.

The main American titles – *Seinfeld, Friends, Ally McBeal, Frasier* – refer not to social castes but to individuals, and none of them relies on a closed milieu for their humour or pathos. Their vision of society is open rather than closed, horizontal rather than vertical, actual rather than nostalgic. For all these reasons they tend to be wittier, more sophisticated, better written, more intelligent and with a sharper contemporary edge. New types, such as the dysfunctional psychiatrist in *Frasier*, the big city inadequates in *Seinfeld*, or the loopy female lawyer in *Ally McBeal* are preferred to cosy images of dinner ladies and other reach-me-down, sentimentalized characters, often Northern, on which audiences seem to dote. The shame of it is that, when we aspire to something less conventional – *Absolutely Fabulous* or the satire of inverted racism by Ali G – the talent appears and the script crackles.

Populist snobbery amongst British TV writers and producers is rife. Advising new writers to avoid anything middle class, the highly successful screenwriter Jimmy McGovern said: 'You've got to have stories to tell, and you don't get the great stories from the safe lives of the middle classes.' No Marxist theoretician would have swept George Eliot, Dostoyevsky and Flaubert into the dustbin of history so disdainfully.

The fact that the American sense of equality is more natural, more in the bone, does not guarantee fine works of contemporary literature or first-rate sitcoms: it just makes them possible. And, of course, everything has its downside. One result of America's inbred egalitarian sense is that populism can be even more crass over there than over here, as anyone who has found themselves mesmerized by the inanities of American TV at its worst will know. Instead of being coy or condescending, the appeal to brute tastes is naked and unabashed. To that extent it is also more honest. And because Americans are less haunted by social considerations than ourselves there are more free spirits, and their best artists and creators fall less predictably into self-consciously anti-elite stances. Maybe this is why, at their peaks, both their popular and literary culture are currently more impressive than our own, the popular more vital and inventive, the literature on a higher plane.

Culture in Britain is immersed in a swamp of non-aesthetic anxieties and concerns. The very terms 'culture' or 'the arts' induce a strange schizophrenia. On the one hand we feel obliged to be solemn and reverential (art, the new religion); at the same time we feel we must jolly the people along by insisting that the arts can be fun. All this leads to a tormented way of talking. When the subject is culture, only in Britain is it possible to sound high falutin' and ingratiating, patrician and deferential, up-tight and anti-elitist at one and the same time. If the orations of arts ministers or officials are notable for their intricate balances and tortured phrasing, it is because they are both pronouncements of authority and a form of plea-bargaining with the masses. The fact that in socially transvestite Britain the elites masquerade as the masses does not make the drafting easier.

Gerry Robinson, a New Labour magnifico, is both Chairman of the Arts Council and Chairman of the Granada entertainment group. The fact that he is also a government appointee makes him a one-man synthesis of the new elites, who brings together the commercial, cultural and political strands. Anti-elitism is consequently his leitmotiv:

Too often in the past, the arts have taken a patronizing attitude to audiences. Too often artists and performers have continued to ply their trade to the same white, middle-class audience. In the back of their minds lurks the vague hope that one day enlightenment might descend semi-miraculously upon the rest, that the masses might get wise to their brilliance . . . (*An Arts Council for the Future*, 1998)

Intellectually Mr Robinson has here performed a criminal act. In a single brief passage he derided the accomplishment of artists and performers, scorned the cultural tastes of the white middle classes, which is to say some 80 per cent of his countrymen, and made obsequious noises before people he erroneously thinks of as the masses. Yet we forgive him, since he clearly had no idea what he was doing. It would be fruitless to attempt to explain his crime to him. This would involve him stepping outside the self-gratifying world of conventional thinking, which commercially and politically successful egalitarian elites have absolutely no incentive to do.

His is a shining instance of a *de haut en bas* stance towards the public cloaked in the velvet tones of ultra-democracy. He speaks of a patronizing attitude: what he could never be brought to understand is that it is he who is the patron. The dictionary definition is 'one who stands to another in relations analogous to those of a father; a lord or master, a protector'. With his political, cultural and commercial powers and paternalist posture, that would seem a neat description of Robinson. It is not the artists and performers who are patronizing audiences by expecting them to 'get wise to' what he sardonically calls their brilliance. It is he, in his self-appointed role of lord protector of the masses, who is suggesting that brilliance in art is an elitist chimera, and in any case it is not for them.

Inverted elites are intent on something that it would never occur to men and women of any genuine cultural understanding to do: to narrow or eliminate differences between various forms of art. Like the most fatuous of snobs they are mesmerized by status, interested in nothing but social tone. Except in the minds of those who approach culture from a political or ideological viewpoint, the question of the status of art, the high and the low of it, is a pseudo-problem. The highs and lows lie mainly in the level of achievement in the genre, and many (the author included) would claim that the best of popular culture is currently at something of a high in aesthetic terms.

In their truthfulness, originality, invention, artistry, wit and technical brilliance, the outstanding films, cartoons and sitcoms of our time frequently soar higher than the allegedly high art of a big-name novel or a poor, pretentious play. To watch the cartoon or sitcom, scripted by people no one has heard of, rather than sitting down to the over-puffed novel or going to the must-see play (which statisticians will log as cultural activities) can frequently turn out to be a discerning choice. Such is our concern for status that if the script of the (usually American) sitcom were to be Anglicized, signed by a celebrity and clapped between hardback covers it would be greeted by critics as a major contribution to the English comic novel. Similarly the best advertising can be superior to the witless japes and nihilistic posturing of much contemporary art. Each is ephemeral, but the advertising at least has a purpose, as well as fewer illusions about its status as art.

Fine work with a wide appeal can flourish without the patronage of inverted elites. Popular culture at its best needs no defence and no condescension. All that is needed is for bad popular culture to be criticized as vigorously as bad high art. Inverted elites are patronizing in a void: there is no height to patronize from and no low to condescend to. End of problem.

Though not for government. New Labour's earnest patronage of mass culture is equalled only by the earnestness of its resolve to ensure that the other sort of culture is presented in such a way as to make it accessible to mass audiences. The result can be language reminiscent of the Five Year Plan. Announcing 'a new watchdog' for the cultural and sporting fields, Chris Smith, the Culture Secretary, said in December 1998: 'We will give direction. We shall set targets and chase progress, and where appropriate we will take direct action to make sure that our objectives are achieved.' A year later he wrote: 'I believe strongly that enhancing the cultural and creative life of the nation is a key function of government. And this is not just by boosting investment, but also by giving strategic direction and encouraging progress towards clear objectives.'

Direct action, key government functions, strategic direction, enhancing our creative lives, progress towards clear objectives in the arts – these are stonily bureaucratic and grossly Philistine phrases. Until recently it would not have been possible for any minister of culture to talk like this: to do so implies a degree of centralized planning that would have been seen as, if not quasi-totalitarian, at least authoritarian. The idea that the soft-mannered Smith might be metamorphosing before our eyes into a British Zhdanov (Stalin's notorious arts minister in the 1940s) is inherently comical, but soft manners can go with soft thinking, and Smith is an example of the sentimental fervour that can seize inverted elites where culture is concerned. His determination to brook no opposition in his campaign to bring culture to the people displays an ingenuousness which, though touching in its way, can have its dangers.

I am not alone in having noted this trend. A remarkable analysis by Andrew Brighton, a critic and curator at the Tate Gallery, entitled *Towards a Command Culture*, dissects the Government's cultural policy by reference to Soviet Socialist Realism. I repeat, no one is calling anyone a communist, and Brighton is careful to indicate the limits of his analogy. Yet ideas about culture blur and converge at the edges, especially when they are as mistily conceived as those of Chris Smith, and Brighton's central thesis is convincing: that the autonomy of the state-supported arts is being eaten away as the government increasingly sees them as an instrument of social policy.

The main components of Soviet arts policy were *narodnost'*, *klassovost'* and *partiinost'* – 'peopleness' (not populism, but rooted in the people), class content and a party mission. In spongy form all three can be found in New Labour's cultural programme. Brighton concludes:

What seems to be implied and enacted by the present government's cultural policy is that certain social goals and political aims are so self-evidently good that subordinating much of publicly supported arts culture to them is justified. It seems we are seeing the tragedy of Soviet Socialist Realism replayed as a social democratic farce . . . The overt government demand on the arts is that they serve everyone and foster shared values in the name of social inclusion. The covert effect is to demote not just dissenting culture but also aesthetic integrity.

I do not for a moment suppose that the Government aims to demote dissenting culture in the Soviet sense. But it has made its 'strategic direction' for culture clear, and arts bureaucracies react to government policies like any other: they not only follow their masters' wishes, they demonstrate their loyalty by anticipating them. In planning their programmes they will read the runes and make their calculations. The word will go out that museums, theatres and galleries who attract audiences by popular rather than over-demanding shows will get more subsidies than those who do not. And as in authoritarian regimes there will be excesses of zeal by apparatchiks keen to promote their careers by demonstrating their affection for the people in deed as in word. The most alarming aspect of this policy of populist preference is not that it is conducted in secret; it is that it is pursued openly. Recently, for example, Sadler's Wells Opera was informed that if it wanted more cash from the state its performances should be less 'purist'.

In a true democracy it is not the job of ministers to lay down strategic directions for the arts, and certainly not to approve or disapprove of this or that opera, novel, play or film; for that we have audiences and professional critics. But ultra-democracies are driven by different imperatives, and when they announce a strategic plan to bring culture to the masses they are likely to have decided ideas about what sort of culture it should be. Smith may achieve his numbers, or even, as the Russian Five Year planners habitually did, triumphantly exceed them. But increasingly his success is likely to be at the cost of artistic integrity and independence. The result of Socialist Realism, implemented in a police state, was lugubrious works sanctifying the proletariat. The results of 'art for the many, not for the few', implemented by smiley apparatchiks, could be museums transformed into fairgrounds and lugubriously jollified opera. More fun for the masses, perhaps, though in aesthetic terms often pretty much on a par.

The logic of ultra-democracy in the arts is simple. Now that the old elites are vanquished or on the retreat the creative energies of the people are finally released. Providing enough money and facilities are forthcoming, the arts can do no other than to flourish in every domain. It may indeed be that a new arts complex permits a promising piece of experimental theatre to be successfully performed, or the staging of a high quality exhibition that attracts large crowds. Yet to what end the new facilities for the arts are devoted, like the quality of the steel produced in Five Year Plans (it was often deficient), can become a secondary consideration.

Increasingly the pressure is for the productions to be, in that tautological yet heavily freighted phrase, 'audience focused'. As so often with this kind of jargon the concept is sentimental, and goes back to Rousseau's *Lettre Sur Les Spectacles*. Here he begins by deploring the isolation of the individual in his aesthetic pleasure, and the gap between audience and performers, and ends by doing away with theatre altogether: 'What shall be the objects of the spectacle? Nothing, if you so wish . . . Better still, let the spectators partake of the spectacle, make them actors themselves, let each person see himself and love himself in others, and they will be the more closely united.' Such is the somewhat crazed theory. In practice, when the audience begins to matter more than the performance, arts bureaucracies, for all their high-minded protestations, are merely echoing the values of commerce.

The reluctance of ministers of culture and their officials to question the quality of the return on their 'investment in the arts' (another Philistine expression) contrasts with Government practice in other fields. Ministers of health confess to short-comings in the NHS and chivvy those responsible. The Chancellor of the Exchequer makes speeches to the CBI admitting that our productivity is way behind that of the Germans or Americans, that our old industrial sector is superannuated and that our new technologies are lagging. Imagine a minister of culture suggesting that there might be something not quite up to scratch in our films, our music – pop or classical – our drama, our contemporary arts, our sitcoms or our pottery, or that our competitors were outsmarting us. On the contrary, officialdom is invariably excited and delighted, in veritable burbles of ravishment, at everything that is happening in the arts.

The visual arts are often said to give us a premonition of the way the world is tending. As a scratch theory it has the virtue of appearing to work. In their immediacy, their sensuous appeal, their insistence that we look and the ease of looking, the visual arts, above all other genres, give us the feeling of being 'of the time'. The stabbing brushstrokes of David now seem to have announced the Terror (in which the artist was to play an inglorious part). The stone-dead, derivative styles of Victorian art (the Pre-Raphaelites, the mock-classical, the mock-Gothic, the mock-Japanese) announced the frozen antiquarianism of the era. The fragmentation of Russian painting in Malevich and Kandinsky appeared to herald the Revolution, the grotesques and violence of Expressionism pre-figured fascism and Warhol portended the bland indifference of the consumer age.

What does the 'explosion of creativity in British art', heralded by the cultural anti-elites, portend? The question invites a sigh. The reason discussion of the contemporary visual arts tends to be predictable is that it is dominated by the cultural equivalent of up/down thinking. Old v. new, traditional v. modern, reactionaries v. progressives – such false categories, as tired as they are meaningless, pre-empt debate.

The only thing at issue is the quality of the art. We all have our views. What is conventionally called avant-garde art seems to me to have enjoyed a brief but brilliant period in the early decades of the twentieth century. Once it was innovative, witty, intelligent and genuinely troubling, not least by its associations with the universal scientific Utopias of communism or the violence and irrationalism of fascism. Today the question mark over allegedly avant-garde work no longer concerns its legitimacy as art: it is its authenticity on any level. No expert of any repute has much to say in favour of Britart or allied styles. Bryan Robertson, a leading modernist and former director of the Whitechapel Gallery, has described the activities of its prime promoter, Charles Saatchi, as 'coldly speculative' (*Modern Painters*). Of equivalent work in New York, Robert Hughes wrote in his book *American Visions*: 'It affords the pleasure of striking radical attitudes without the risk entailed in radical belief.'

Why, then, discuss it? Because Britart is the official aesthetic of the new elites, and the most powerful symbol of our culture of pretence. There are good reasons why a dated, highly derivative style should find favour with the new patricians. Patricians ancient and modern have one foot in the past, and the *passé* nature of the contemporary avant-garde is central to its appeal to the Establishment. For them the main attraction of Britart is its innocuousness. No ruling caste embraces art forms that pose a threat to it, and the fact that avant-garde art is in an advanced state of decay renders it safe to patronize. Britart is a rusted bomb, retrieved long after the war is over, buffed up and placed on display to give us a retrospective *frisson*. It looks like the genuine thing but it is perfectly safe to handle: the explosive has been removed and the bomb prudently defused some decades ago.

Far from undermining convention, contemporary art is an example of the strain of conservatism and nostalgia in our culture. Britart is a reactionary movement, in the dictionary definition of the term: 'a desire to return to a previous condition of affairs' (in this case to a time when avant-garde art had meaning). Our national proclivity for reinventing the past and re-staging its battles is well documented. In the mid nineteenth century the elites of the time mounted medieval tournaments, mock-Gothic affairs where knights pretended to fight and maidens to be won. In the early twentieth century we reproduced late Impressionism and Post-Impressionism in the gauche and tardy pastiches of Bloomsbury. And today we have caught up with what was once called modern art almost a century after the movement began. As Gore Vidal remarked, everything changes except the avant-garde.

It is sometimes claimed that the contemporary avant-garde should be viewed as a continuation of an honourable tradition. On that account Clement Greenberg, modernism's most discerning theoretician, had this to say in *Partisan Review* as early as 1939:

... This is what is really meant when it is said that the popular art and literature of today were once the daring, esoteric art and literature of yesterday. Of course, no such thing is true. What is meant is that when sufficient time has elapsed the new is looted for new 'twists', which are then watered down and served up as kitsch.

Today the 'arts industry' (more Philistinism) has come up with a snappy product, and the once new ideas of Malevich, Duchamp, Picabia or Tristan Tzara are looted for new twists on a daily basis. Industries need customers, profits and a sales promotion staff, and the question for us is: to whom is this kitsch served up, by whom, and with what purpose in mind? The boosting of contemporary art brings together the key members of our anti-elite oligarchy: the state, cultural official-dom, the media and commercial interests. The state is involved through its patronage, both financial (it pays for art schools and subsidizes public galleries) and in the lordly sense of bestowing approval. Commercial interests are involved as market makers and collectors. Arts apparatchiks and the media, where the majority of critics are prudently sympathetic (prudent because, in a debate conducted in old/new terms, there is only one side they can decently be on), act as clerks of the sale.

While politicians of the Left and Right enthuse about the nation's artistic vitality, promoters and collectors talk up the product with a canny commercial eye. There is nothing wrong with their financial interest *per se;* in the past there was no lack of art dealers who were discerning connoisseurs (Vollard and the Post-Impressionists). But that is not what we are seeing in the promotion of British contemporary art. Charles Saatchi is an advertising man. Lord Palumbo, another apologist for the genre, appointed Chairman of the Arts Council by a Conservative government, is a property developer with a taste for Mies van der Rohe. When admen and property men who rose to prominence in the 'go for it' eighties fasten on to a trend, and the trend is towards the allegedly subversive and anarchic, one begs leave to examine the aesthetic integrity of their intentions. They may see themselves as belonging to that tradition, but Pope Julius II or Charles I of England our new patrons of the arts are not.

Saatchi and Palumbo describe our contemporary artists as new and exciting, terms they might equally apply to a marketing campaign or to a novel method of financing a property deal. (The fact that Charles Saatchi collected contemporary works as well as being a partner in the firm that did the advertising campaign for Margaret Thatcher's election sums up the mock-subversive nature of Britart rather neatly.) Displays are frequently promoted in fairground terms – shocking, funny, irreverent, quirky, grotesque or obscene. Some of it can indeed be mildly amusing, in a lumbering way, though none of it has the wit, intelligence, savvy or craftsmanship of the best TV entertainment. Instead it relies heavily on incongruity, like a schoolboy expletive in adult surroundings, and on a literal-mindedness and anecdotalism that are so often the bane of English art: like the thumping moralism of much Victorian painting, Tracey Emin's bed must tell a story. As such the work is not hard to assimilate, and to judge by exhibition attendances and sales the public are beginning to respond to the promotional activity and media hype.

The selling of 'sensationalist' art to a mass audience is a revealing instance of new elite condescension. Cultural condescension is different from other brands. In this case the patron may or may not be in a position to patronize, since it is by no means certain that he or she is more cultivated than those they play down to. Quite possibly they aren't. Palumbo's famous speech in defence of originality in the arts was a classic of its type. Presenting the Turner Prize, he claimed that Turner was amongst many brilliant artists derided in their time. 'The dunces will always mock the innovator.' Turner's later work was indeed criticized, but his pictures were in high demand during his lifetime; Ruskin, the most revered critic of the period, dedicated a book to him. Who is the Ruskin of Britart? In any case, the implication that, because a famous innovative artist was once criticized, anyone who describes himself as an inno-vator and is mocked deserves to be regarded as a famous artist, is Artworld logic: three men wear red socks, so anyone in red socks is a man.

Palumbo's gaffe was a reminder that the new elites span the political firmament. Here was a Tory and a Lord, with a grave regard for the muses ('The arts speak', he ventured on another occasion, 'of abiding matters'), projecting himself as a defender of revolutionary art. As chairman of the Arts Council at the time of his lapse, his purpose was presumably to jolly the populace through the turnstiles of exhibitions of contemporary work.

No doubt he was sincere in his admiration for the allegedly avant-garde, though one suspects that, as a businessman, he was anxious above all to present himself as modern. Artworld has more than its share of such figures. The governors of the Tate Gallery include four bankers, one ex-diplomat and a former county council official. No doubt they are persons of quality, yet there are two things that, as a caste, our bankers and diplomats and public servants are most unlikely to possess: discriminating knowledge about modern art and a taste for revolution. Patrons in previous centuries (the Church, the state, the aristocracy) supported the art of their time for its celebration of themselves (papal or royal portraits, aristocrats in their rural habitats) or for its religious or patriotic messages. Today the governors of the Tate preside over an institution whose contemporary works (ostensibly) deride or negate all they stand for, and representatives of the political and financial Establishment warmly recommend to the public works that are billed as anti-Establishment art.

In a sense there is no reason for surprise. In Britain few things are quite what they seem. If something looks like a bull, walks like a bull and bellows like a bull, it is very likely a frog. The worthies of Artworld are merely playing their parts in our culture of pretence. We pretend that the nineties were the sixties, that Oasis are The Beatles, that Stephen Fry is Oscar Wilde, that Ken Livingstone is John Wilkes, that Margaret Thatcher is Winston Churchill, that Damien Hirst is Duchamp, that Lord Leighton was a painter and that Vaughan Williams and Elgar, some of whose music Neville Cardus compared to St Pancras station, were composers of global stature. And we go through the motions of believing that the English novel and English poetry are on an historic high, in much the same way that we make believe that a modest terraced house in a London backstreet is worth three quarters of a million dollars. Should anyone question whether these things are actually true, he or she will be reviled from all sides, since the make-believe is communal: both Labour and the Tories, for example, share an interest in pretending that Tony Blair is a socialist.

Britart is merely the latest event in our national harlequinade, an anti-authority charade in which the authorities put themselves up for a bit of ragging, and pretend it is real. Their behaviour is reminiscent of school fêtes where the children are invited to smash crockery or hurl flour at teachers. All good fun, no one hurt – indeed the teachers increase their standing in their pupils' eyes by showing what good sports they are. If our cultural *nomenklatura* tolerate and encourage this simulacrum of revolt it is not, as they claim, in the name of artistic freedom: it is because genuine innovation can be powerful and disruptive, whereas Britart kitsch is a product of the system. Alternatively they resort to the post-modernist let-out clause, saying that the art should not be treated too earnestly and is simply to be enjoyed. Either way there are problems of authenticity. If it is insurrectionary art, how is it that the authorities embrace it? And if it is ironic humour, it is an old joke laboriously re-told, with the punch-line missing.

'The King's new clothes', it has been said of the genre, but Britart is more like the King's old clothes: the remnants of twentieth-century modernism passed down like cast-offs to the people. The fact that the Serpentine Gallery (former patron, Princess Diana) and the Royal Academy specialize in the more sensationalist types of art is symbolic – as neat an example of inverted elites at work as one could wish for. Anti-monarchists might go further, noting perhaps a concordance between the meretricious aspect of contemporary royalty and the trashiness of much contemporary art.

Galleries are proliferating throughout the country, notably in the north. It would be easy to write off such places as palaces of fun for the Sunday masses, if the implications were not rather more serious. I do not mean their low educational value, though the books and brochures that accompany such exhibitions are on a desolating intellectual level. (On the poverty of academic publications in the field Sir Ernst Gombrich has remarked: 'The progress of modern science is so enormous that I am a little embarrassed when I see my university colleagues discussing genetic codes, while the art historians discuss the fact that Duchamp sent a *pissoir* to an exhibition.') Nor do I have in mind the cost, though that is colossal, and the money could be better used in our schools, perhaps in promoting a better grounding in the history of the visual arts.

What I mean are the ethics. There is something morally distasteful about publicly financed institutions attempting to attract a new and probably inexperienced public to art of seriously questionable quality that claims to 'challenge the system'. Like all elites the gallery directors or curators are often insufficiently self-critical, and their mindset too conventional, to ask themselves what they are about. ('Artworld', wrote Robert Hughes, 'makes no critique of its criticism.') How does one explain to such people that they *are* the system, and that their young visitors are its victims? Elite nineteenth-century figures, such as Prince Albert, an earnest social improver who insisted that the museums he founded should be free, were unashamedly didactic: to educate the tastes and raise the aspirations of the common man, in the bourgeois mould. For all their paternalism, pomposity and blinkered vision, at least they were honest.

'Agitated and monotonous.' That, Tocqueville warned, could be the fate of the democracies of the future. At times his words appear to apply to pretty well every area of modern life: obviously to politics, certainly the media, most definitely pop music. Yet one hesitates to complain. If pop is the music of the times, objecting to it would be like objecting to the age in which we live. Criticizing pop is like railing against the atmosphere: you may fear for your lungs, but there is nothing else to breathe, and improvements in the short term do not seem likely.

Whatever is said or not said, the rock industry or something like it will continue to thrive. This is because pop music satisfies the two basic needs of the mass society: the useful and the popular. It is popular because its star system carries echoes of folk heroes, however travestied by commercialism and the celebrity culture; because its gilded and spangled idols relieve the drabness of democracy; and because its most able performers can hit upon an appealing melody or clever lyrics. And it is useful because, however good or bad the music, the beat provides something to dance to, and its volume has an anaesthetizing quality.

Pop is the court music of ultra-democracy, and its singers and players enjoy high official favour. Its attractions to the new elites are obvious. For politicians, pop is an entry point into the affections of the young, and of people they persist in thinking of as the masses. To business and the media it signifies vast spending power. And to the arts establishment it offers that inestimable prize, something to condescend to. Best of all for these men and women of power, who tend to be of a certain age and from sedate, upper-middling backgrounds, pop music offers safely packaged dissent. The attitudes of the suave politico, the wily broadsheet editor or eagerly appreciative arts official towards the latest hit single are correspondingly indulgent. The minister respectfully requests the presence of pop's biggest stars at his parties, the 'qualities' give it as much or more space than the traditional arts and the Arts Council and Lottery Commission subsidize a flourishing multi-billion-pound private industry by providing public money for, amongst other things, a pop museum.

Since none of the above is likely to care anything for the music, the fact that their patronage compromises its authenticity and deadens its vitality is of no consequence. Expert critics are aware of what is going on. Simon Napier-Bell, one-time manager of the Yardbirds, T-Rex, Japan and Wham!, is without illusions:

No more Cold War; no more apartheid; peace in Ireland; agreement in the Middle East – we are living in a consensual age . . . What's good for world peace is lousy for the rock business. When it started in the 1950s rock was instantly political. You pushed your arse into tight leather jeans and shoved your credentials into the audience's face. Jumping around with a guitar was enough to show dissatisfaction with the *status quo* . . .

Throughout the 1970s and 1980s, with the continued use of drugs, pop and rock artists retained their image of being on the fringes of society. And as long as Thatcher was in power they kept themselves latently political . . . But Blair has finished that off. Youth culture is no longer feared by the establishment. It receives grants. Aspiring pop stars can sign on the dole, while they learn their trade and wait to be discovered. This is not good for rock music. Before they can spit them angrily in our faces young people are having their grievances removed. And if they manage to find something to rile about they are listened to sympathetically and sent for counselling . . . This is not temporary. The rock era has come and gone, along with political polarization and the generation gap. It has been replaced by kitsch pop, as stimulating as sucking a Murray Mint. (*LM Magazine*)

Sam Taylor, another commentator on pop, is similarly trenchant: 'The Government approves of it, the media consumes it voraciously, museums are erected in its honour. But there is something rotten in the state of pop.'

Taylor and Napier-Bell have spotted the source of the rot. Official patronage of 'protest art' blunts its blade; the one sure thing about the 'cutting edge' culture vaunted by the Government and the media, in art or music or theatre, is that no blood will flow. Yet no one can give up the pretence. If there were no pop, what would there be? We can only suspend our disbelief and clap along. When the state and society applaud the assault on their nominally conservative values by nominal anti-elites, the result is a double imposture, as synthetic insubordination encounters synthetic tolerance. It is that which is rotten.

An evasive or insinuating stance towards pop is frequent amongst writers and intellectuals. When Salman Rushdie published a book about rock singers, *The Ground Beneath Her Feet*, accompanied by a pop CD, the critics were divided; those in favour often acclaimed the book for what one suspects were not purely literary reasons. At the same time Rushdie wrote an article in *Prospect* magazine lamenting that, in an age when rock has become middle-aged and corporate, its oppositional origins are forgotten, and confessed to his nostalgia: 'for popular music fans of a certain age the ideas of rock and revolution are inseparable'. A banal enough observation, one might think; what more natural than for the middle-aged to recall the glory days of rock with the escapist's sigh of 'those were the days'? The trouble is that those were never the days. To suggest that rock and revolution remain inseparable is deeply self-deluding. They weren't then and they are most certainly not now. The assimilation of pop music by the Establishment began early; that is why ageing rockers tend to be rich. The Labour prime minister Harold Wilson received The Beatles in Number 10, just as Tony Blair was to receive their mimics, the leaders of Oasis, thirty years later. It is rock and the *status quo* that have proved inseparable.

Rushdie recounts that his faith in rock was revived by President Havel, who told him that its role in the velvet revolution and the collapse of communism could not be overstated. Havel's point – that young people in totalitarian regimes envied the liberty enjoyed by their counterparts in capitalist countries to express themselves and their discontents through music, and that their envy fuelled dissent – is incontrovertible, though clearly overstated, possibly to flatter Rushdie. It is equally incontrovertible that in their youthful romanticism, the majority of Western rock musicians favoured unilateral nuclear disarmament. To say that the protests of pop musicians played a role in bringing the Vietnam War to an end is an arguable thesis. To suggest that they helped to end the Cold War is not. Had the West one-sidedly abandoned its nuclear weapons, it seems reasonable to suppose that communism would have lingered on, perhaps for decades, together with Soviet domination of Czechoslovakia. Similarly, it stretches credulity to suggest, as is sometimes done, that the kind of revolution pop fans saw as inseparable from rock was directed as much against the interests of Soviet Russia and China as of the West. If one were being impolite one might even describe such a suggestion as a historical lie; many a rocker saw the murderous Cultural Revolution in China as fabulous. But, of course, we are dealing not with lies, but with nostalgic, self-delusive impostures.

Indulgence towards rock is important because it is symptomatic of the top–down instincts of British literary elites. Major foreign writers do not behave like this. American authors do not patronize pop, they register its ubiquitous presence, a different thing. John Updike and Philip Roth refer to tunes or bands to capture the flavour of an epoch, or set a scene, and as early as 1973 Don DeLillo wrote a witty and perceptive novel, *Great Jones Street*, on the subject. (It is odd that Martin Amis has never turned his satirical talents on that very particular national type, the English pop star.) DeLillo's hero was Bucky Wunderlick, a star who gave it up. Despite sardonic touches ('By the end', Bucky's girlfriend tells him, 'you were making incredible amounts of noise and communicating absolutely nothing'), the novel was not hostile to pop. Though nor was it a multicultural celebration, and certainly not indulgent or sentimental. A hard honest look at the way things tend to be in the pop world, it was received accordingly.

'Luminous' was the verdict of *Village Voice*. 'Finally someone who understands rock and roll! Don DeLillo's third book taps into rock both as overheated romantic myth and useless commodity, art chained to commerce. It's so snappy that the good ideas only kick in afterwards, like good rock and roll.' Both the book and its reception seem grown-up, mature. The thought of top level American writers suggesting that rock was a serious force in ending the Cold War is inconceivable, and would be seen for what it is: achingly condescending. Which all helps to explain why, for all his early promise, Rushdie is not in the league of Roth, Updike or DeLillo. In literature, as in life, condescension is a killer.

Purists like Simon Napier-Bell complain about rock music degenerating into the blandest of kitsch. Maybe so, but kitsch and blandness sell, and pop is expanding its audiences in two directions. Fans now begin in their pre-teens and continue into late middle age – given the music's Murray Mint flavour, an unsurprising span. What is truly extraordinary is that music that appeals to five of the seven ages of man and which swamps the public and commercial airwaves day and night retains its antinomian image. The writer Will Self has said: 'In recent years television and pop music have begun to be made by the people who were its first generation of child consumers, while at the same time the overall population has aged. This phenomenon gives rise to the sense of impacted decadence which permeates our popular culture.' A reasonable point, except that 'phoney' might be a less artful but more honest adjective than 'impacted'. As the nine-year-olds join hands with adolescents, and the adolescents with the over forties, a kind of inter-generational simulacrum of a counter-culture has come about. Three things, it seems to me, can be concluded from the fantasy decadence and theatre of anarchy we hear and see around us, in the media or in pubs and clubs: the power and guile of the pop music industry; the fact that the young and middle-aged each strive towards the sainted status of late adolescence; and the inalienable links between pop and the system. The fact is that mimetic, Murray Mint protest helps keep people sweet.

It is therefore no surprise that authority should extend official support and encouragement to the rock industry, just as it does to the arms trade. Pacifist rock singers and weapons of war are, after all, two of our most thriving exports. Pop music in Britain, like the armaments industry, is acquiring the character of a state/private partnership. The state plays its part by promotion through the British Council, opening up export markets, or awarding funds, local facilities or scholarships. Social security benefits are paid to promising talents in much the way that monarchs once dispensed sinecures to their favourites. And should the musicians bite the hand of their patrons, as some inevitably do, the result can be as entertaining as the music. Noel Gallagher of Oasis, the former guest of Tony Blair in Number 10, said later in an interview: 'Being famous is a good laugh when you're on drugs. You go "Nah, nah, fucking nah" and everyone goes, "Wow, hasn't he got loads of charisma?" And really, you're just hammered' (*Observer*, November 1999).

As the power and prestige of pop wax ever greater, its relation-ship with authority becomes paradoxical. While the new patricians endlessly strive to project a demotic image, pop stars take on the worldly-wise postures and venerable airs of the old elite. Retired or semi-retired rockers are coming to resemble a new aristocracy, and share many of its less endearing features. Like their historical predecessors the balladeers of ultra-democracy are dripping with riches in whose acquisition chance may well have played a greater part than merit: just as the aristocrat chances to be born into the right family, the pop star has the luck to be born with the right personal style at the opportune moment. Lords and rockers are both inclined to affect a languid manner, to see themselves as above conventional morality, to live in luxurious estates, and to exploit their promin-ence in society to propagate quirky or self-interested opinions. Each in his way is a defender of the *status quo*, the rock star having as much interest in destroying the social arrangements that have led to his enrichment and celebrity as the peer in the abolition of the House of Lords. In an ultra-democracy, lords and rockers, stalwarts of the up/down system, have their appointed roles. The parts they play are interdependent, and each shares an interest in keeping things much as they are. For when the last hereditary peer is expelled from the Upper House, bang will go another grievance. (One of the many reasons I favour expulsion.)

A society whose culture becomes a theatre of protest in which the applause of the elites is amongst the heartiest, for all the world as if they were participants in a demonstration against themselves, is without precedent. Yet it seems hard to see why things should change. An ultra-democracy has nowhere to go beyond itself, and ends by treading water, by dancing on the spot. To convince itself that it is dynamic, on the move, driven by creative tensions, it fabricates its own opposition. So we have our multi-millionaire rebels, our mock-subversive art and our illegal substances that everyone takes. For egalitarian elites, pop culture is the contemporary equivalent of cakes and ale. Providing it is widely enough distributed and the clientele is contented, they face no challenge from below to trouble their complacency or to explode their myths. The simulation of dissent is big business, and if the consumers are happy to buy, it is hardly surprising if the elites are keen to take their cut. Seen this way all would seem to be for the best in our culture of pretence.

Contemporary fiction and poetry are generally agreed to be on a higher plane of authenticity than rock music or contemporary art. Yet here, too, intimations of inversion are not uncommon. The death of the Poet Laureate, Ted Hughes, and the search for a successor, showed how literary elites can work themselves into warped and crooked postures. There is a case for having a Poet Laureate, and an even better one (in the author's view) for abandoning the tradition. But that is by the way. If someone is to volunteer for the post, the least one can expect is that he or she should be a supporter of the monarchy. Only in a world of inverted elites, where status-seeking and ambition go hand in hand with anti-Establishment mimes, could we end up with a Poet Laureate who makes a show of his left-wing republican sympathies.

The tale began immediately after Hughes's death. Talented as he was, for a mixture of patriotic and egalitarian reasons (in this case equality with the past), in our inflated literary currency he was bound to be portrayed as something more: one of England's greatest poets, or in some cases one of the finest of all time. His true stature will continue to be debated. What matters here is the choice of his successor. In the discussion of candidates many a literary figure who had puffed Hughes to the skies nevertheless insisted that the next Laureate should be younger and more populist. The eventual choice could scarcely have been more symptomatic of the shift from old to new elites.

Hughes was a respected poet. Andrew Motion, by common consent, is a lesser figure. Hughes was a private man. Motion is an earnest propagandist for his craft, rightly recommending us to read more Keats (though his biography of the poet is markedly inferior to that of either Robert Gittings or W. Jackson Bate). Hughes kept his politics to himself. Motion undertook to incorporate them into his work and, sadly, has kept his promise, losing few opportunities to advertise his views. Hughes was a convinced supporter of the monarchy to whose existence he owed his position as Laureate. Motion is not. He defined his views as follows:

I'm not a completely cut-and-dried republican, but I think there are bad examples of monarchy and good examples of monarchy ... I would like [the government] to move to the left. I think it should stop mucking around in Europe and get in there. I think it's not good enough to just put a few million quid into schools and into the health service and all those basic things. I think it should be millions and millions. I don't care if they tax us more. Not all of us, but those who can afford to pay a bit more. I don't know what we're doing in our foreign policy ... What on earth are we doing sucking up to the United States? We're Europeans. It doesn't mean we have to be horrible to the States, but to party around with them like that is very peculiar. (*The Devil*, May 1999)

The language is more interesting than the sentiments. 'Millions and millions', 'sucking up', 'mucking around', 'be horrible': these are not just imprecise terms for a poet, they are infantile expressions, curiously reminiscent of Violet Elizabeth Bott in *Just William*. It is impossible to imagine any serious writer in any other country discussing politics in these terms. Though Motion's purpose was painfully transparent: having sought and accepted a post about whose legitimacy, being a republican – if not a completely cut-and-dried one – he must entertain doubts, he was displaying his demotic credentials in the way that inverted elites, be they poets, prime ministers or princesses, invariably do. In retrospect it seems almost in anticipation of his appointment that the near-republican should have volunteered some lines to the memory of Diana. His royal preferment secured, he addressed a poem to the TUC.

Cyril Connolly defined the defects of the English novel as thinness of material, poverty of style and lack of power. To these he added a further weakness: 'English novels seem always to be written for superiors or inferiors . . .' Though he exempted some of the works of his time, such as Isherwood's *Mr Norris Changes Trains* and Orwell's *Burmese Days*, it is easy to understand what he meant. Today his remarks, made in 1935, invite the question: has anything changed?

Certainly not the habit of writing down. Two-thirds of a century on, British novelists still seem to find it hard to write eye to eye with the reader. Still there is the feeling that things are never quite on the level, of words and sentiments being pitched at a sloping angle. As in Connolly's day, there are exceptions – J. G. Ballard, Tim Parks, Martin Amis, Penelope Fitzgerald, Tibor Fischer. Yet in their tendency to ingratiate themselves with their readers while elevating themselves above them, a large proportion of our writers fall neatly or slither messily into the category of the new elites. All are convinced humanitarians, which is forgivable, even if their insistence that the world should know it is not. Even when it is well-written the average English novel groans softly but audibly, so as to be sure all can hear, under the burden of its moral feeling. However modern, brash or obscene the style, the effect is curiously lowering, like a bell tolling you to a service in a dour and dowdy church.

A great deal of contemporary British fiction is infused with what might be called genteel moral sentiment. I do not mean that the subjects avoid the raw realities, or that the writing is squeamish or over-delicate. The word 'genteel' comes from 'the gentry', and I use it in its true sense of 'having the habits of a superior station'. Today it is writers, more than churchmen or judges, who are seen as occupying a high moral station in society, and those I have in mind seem anxious to set themselves above us by the superiority of their ethical concerns. As much as to tell a story, their aim appears to be to show themselves as people whose fine feeling and concern for humanity entitle them to a place amongst society's moral elite. When Keats said 'We hate all that has a palpable design on us', he omitted an 'ought'. Unfortunately it seems that readers quite like a hoity-toity moral style, or have been conditioned to accept it (an aspect of our Vicar of Bray deference to whoever is the current gentry, perhaps?).

It is enough to glance at six of the last seven winners of the Booker Prize. Not all, of course, are English, or even British, but they were selected by Britons, and for all the Irish, Scottish or even Indian variations, they conform to what might broadly be called a British style. All are well-written novels, saturated in genteel moral sentiment. Roddy Doyle's *Paddy Clarke Ha Ha Ha* is about a tough Irish childhood, but the children are very nice. The subject of *How Late It Was, How Late* by James Kelman is a blind man scandalously mistreated by the social security and prison services. The hero of Pat Barker's *The Ghost Road* is working class and articulate and intelligent, anti-war but a war hero none the less, and bisexual to boot. Graham Swift chose amiable East-enders as the subject for his *Last*

Orders. The God of Small Things by Arundhati Roy is about a good-natured woman having a love affair with a good-natured lower-caste Indian, and featured more nice children. And though the central character of Ian McEwan's *Amsterdam* isn't nice at all – an ambitious Tory foreign secretary who is a hanger, flogger, racist and adulterer (his only positive quality in new elite eyes is that, in spare moments, he is a cross-dresser) – the author's sentiments towards his anti-hero are morally impeccable. The award of the 1999 Booker Prize to J. M. Coetzee for his *Disgrace*, an implacably honest novel, marked a welcome break with the conscience-fondling tradition.

In all these books someone was having a bad time of it, and in each case a big black cross was marked to indicate where our hearts should lie. Reading such works is like filling out a questionaire under the gaze of ethical inquisitors. The question the authors seem implicitly to be asking is 'Are your moral sentiments functioning as they should? Tell me, when did you last pass a tear?' I realize the same could be said of the creator of Tiny Tim or Little Nell, but that in a way is my point. At the heart of many a fearsomely contemporary English novel lies a strain of Victorian moralizing and sentimentalism.

We feel *obliged* to like books high on genteel moral sentiment in the way the Victorians were *obliged* to feel they were enjoying their Sunday sermons: because they are good for us. In our more sententious novelists, echoes of the chapbook and the chapel are never far away. Perhaps all this is inevitable in a secular age. T. E. Hulme described Romanticism as spilt religion, and today the spillage has become a flood. Art is our surrogate faith, so it is natural that the fiction of the most irreligious country in Europe should be awash with humanitarian admonition. In literature the new elites are also the new divines, who can rely for commendation on a coterie of pietistic critics. Selecting Graham Swift's *Last Orders* as one of the fifty best novels of the century (a self-conscious gesture of anti-elite defiance in itself), John Carey wrote in *The Sunday Times*:

Shakespeare occasionally gives lower-class characters speeches that shame the high-ups by their gentleness or nobility. But here the effect is carried through a whole book. Cockney speech becomes a vehicle for nuance and tenderness. If a language reflects the temper of its people, we should be proud of this book's language – or proud of the generation, now passing, that spoke it.

Parsonical echoes linger beyond the final sentence, and after a short silence we half expect a 'let us pray'. In populist democracies literary criticism can come to resemble *Thought for the Day*. Carey's praise for East-enders oozes condescension. Whoever supposed for a second that Cockney speech was incapable of being a vehicle for nuance and tenderness? And why limit our pride in humanity to a generation, now passing, of Cockneys? What is so distinctive about them? Are we implying that the dialect of Mandarin spoken in the Chinese province of Anhui or, come to that, the dialect of any region and language you care to name, may be incapable of expressing such feelings?

American writing, God knows, has its own version of genteel moral sentiment. The difference is that one finds not a drop of it in their most celebrated authors or critics. The comparison with recent Booker winners is, of course, somewhat arbitrary, but Philip Roth, Saul Bellow, John Updike, Robert Stone, Thomas Pynchon, Don DeLillo or Norman Mailer do not present us with characters on whom we are invited to shower our protective feelings from a social or moral height. (In DeLillo's *Underground*, incidentally, J. Edgar Hoover, a real-life far-right politician who also happened to be a cross-dresser, gets infinitely subtler treatment than McEwan's flimsy monster. The American is not concerned with telling us how high-minded he is about people like Hoover, any more than he was to tell us, in *Great Jones Street*, how much he approved of rock. He sees and presents his characters sideways on. This is what I mean by writing on the level.)

The tendency of many of our authors to adopt shared stances

or to congeal into cliques is symptomatic of our mania for conformity and stratification. Again there are exceptions, but our literary elites, like all superior castes, tend to have a set view of society. Everyone to his or her box. Such is the compulsion towards orthodoxy, and the rigour of inverted codes, that when they find a niche, they stick to it. The result can be damaging to the work of able writers. The arty lesbianism into which Jeanette Winterson has lapsed is taking its toll of her once outstanding talents, just as the social anarchism of Irvine Welsh, powerful in his earlier work, is becoming increasingly sophomoric: a dismal example of a writer growing into immaturity as he burrows ever deeper into his box.

Cliquishness and conformism extend to politics. One might have thought that the political opinions of fiction writers, should they feel obliged to have them, would reflect their differing experiences, personalities, convictions and imaginations. At the very least we feel we have a right to variety. Ah for an author who is an anarchist, a Trotskyite, a Christian, a Seventh Day Adventist, a far-rightist even! But no: our highly conventionalized elites present us with a pro-forma model, and to judge from their utterances and their works there are few British writers who would not sign up to Andrew Motion's statement of beliefs, with the necessary improvements to the language. It is not the beliefs that are shocking, it is their predictability.

If a selection of our novelists were to gather for a weekend seminar on social and political affairs ('The writer's engagement with society'), the proceedings would be brief. An identity of views would be reached over coffee on morning one, upon which the seminar would be free to disperse, after a statement to the press recording their warm solidarity on all major questions of the day. The liberal press would welcome them as the conscience of the nation, the right-wing press would denounce them as a covey of luvvies and everyone would be content. So it goes in the up/down society.

In France or America, where literary elites are less cohesive, it is hard to picture this happening. Amongst major American authors no easy identity of views would appear to exist. In so far as their positions are evident from their work, not a few would seem to be cultural conservatives and political agnostics. The seminar might be hard to get together at all, as the better-known writers, fearing attempts to dragoon them into regimented postures, declined to attend. Were they nevertheless to be persuaded to put in a show, this gathering too might disperse after coffee, due to a reluctance to pronounce on policy matters outside the writer's direct province, to irreconcilable differences if they tried or to a punch-up provoked by Norman Mailer. As for the French, in the Sartrean era there would have been little difficulty in filling the seminar room, or a conference hall. Today the majority of writers might leave the invitation unanswered, on the grounds that they were too busy trying to rescue the French novel from oblivion, and that all that socio-political stuff was a long, long time ago.

In an ultra-democracy, status matters. The paradox should not surprise us: the price of equality, Rousseau foresaw, can be a preoccupation with rank and degree. A distinguishing feature of British writing and criticism is a preoccupation with the literary status of individual authors or their works. Not too many authors seem content. Literary writers (the phrase is hotly resented by genre writers) tend to feel that their incomes are out of sync with their talents, and in the case of less instantly accessible authors this can often be the case. For popular authors the grievance is the reverse: multi-millionaires they may frequently be, but this is small solace for their failure to feature in the contemporary canon. So we have the spectacle of authors of spy thrillers, sex-laden dramas or journalistic novels coming together, in a sort of trade union of the stinkingly rich and terminally disgruntled, to denounce what they see as the artificial division between best-selling and literary novels.

The grievance of the multi-millionaires is deeply felt. Writers like Robert Harris, Ken Follett and John le Carré have each found ways to imply that it is only the snobbery of the literary Establishment which prevents them being accorded the repute they merit. Such authors seem to see themselves as victims of their success: the fact that their books are read by large numbers of people is, in their eyes, a black mark against them. When literary works of dubious distinction are talked up by critics or awarded prizes because the critics or judges are striving for a popular image, it becomes easy to sympathize with the genre writers' frustration. They see no great difference between the 'literary' works and their own, and they are right. Yet in general their demands are suspect. As in art or popular music, those whose main appeal is to mass markets want it all ways: the breaking down of hierarchies and the raising of their works to the highest status. In literature this means the elevation of the middle-brow and accessible to *primus inter pares* in a class-free world of letters.

We have reached a point of cultural inversion where popular authors denounce the habit of relegating their writings to the realms where they belong as elitism, while literary writers ache for popular status and the income that goes with it. The parallels with politics are striking. Just as a lifetime's opposition to the antiquated flummery of the House of Lords has not prevented self-proclaimed socialists from dressing up as required, so middle- or low-brow authors cling to their sales and celebrity while simultaneously pining to be decked in literary ermine. As always, denunciations of the old elite are accompanied by an unseemly haste to step into their shoes.

The tendency spans literature and the media, and as the trajectories of Lord Archer and Waheed Alli (a multi-millionaire TV entrepreneur, now also a peer) show, when it comes to making a career in the masses, party preferences are of small importance. The careers of the two men – except, of course, for Archer's brushes with the law – have developed in neat parallel. Archer made his fortune writing popular novels. Alli made his on TV, especially *The Big Breakfast*, which gave Chris Evans his start. Archer was a fundraiser for the Tories, Alli gave generously to Labour. And both were awarded a place in the House of Lords. It is a milestone in the development of ultra-democracy, and a sign of the irresistible ascendency of the new elites, when a writer of Archer's quality is sent to the Upper House, while a TV mogul whose distinctions include furthering the career of the stupendously successful and mesmerically talent-free Chris Evans is also solemnly inducted into the Lords.

In each case their fortunes have been built on selling the lowest form of culture to the largest number of people. There is nothing wrong with that: it has always happened, and in America it is much the same. Yet there is a crucial difference. In America populist writers and the owners of down-market TV channels must content themselves with their fame and their wealth. In status-obsessed Britain, vulgarity not only pays, it is ennobled.

The way out of these dilemmas seems clear. As in the high/low art debate, the best solution to a pseudo-problem is: just don't think about it. But 'it' means rank and degree, and not thinking about it is the one thing an ultra-democracy, hag-ridden by anxieties about class and caste, cannot do. Whether they are looking down or up, spooning with the masses or hoisting themselves on their shoulders, for our elite egalitarians, in one form or another 'it' haunts their every waking hour.

A feature of old-style elites was their patriotism. In eras of peace this took the form not of outright nationalism (our very tolerance of foreigners was a sign of superiority), but of complacent insularity. Complacency, by definition, is resistant to change, and the comfort we derive from being ourselves constantly finds new forms of expression. Beneath the upheavals and agitations of the last few decades lay an incurable self-contentment, evident in every era from Macmillan through Harold Wilson and James Callaghan to Thatcher and Tony

Blair. 'You've never had it so good', said Macmillan to a nation visibly on the slide. Harold Wilson never thought much of abroad, and was not inclined to discover anything about it. 'Crisis? What crisis?' was the tenor of Callaghan's response when, in the late seventies, we had reached a low point in post-war history. Thatcher with her fantasy of Britain as the offshore Hong Kong of Europe, Major with his appeal for an already easeful people to feel at ease with themselves, Blair with his unctuous intimations of moral superiority – the work of our prime ministers in confirming us in our self-satisfaction is never done.

The same complacency was there in the long unquestioned wisdom of our constitution, with its not-to-be bettered triumvirate of the Monarchy, the Commons and the House of Lords – each now in crisis of varying severity. In education it was there in our pride in our primary schools, now finally acknowledged as the primary source of our national under-achievement. It was there in the conceit that British justice, unlike its natural inferiors abroad, did not make mistakes. And till recently it was there in the touchingly parochial notion that we should be proud of the NHS, even if it didn't work, because the benighted citizenry of other Western nations had no health service at all. The ostrich (to borrow Arthur Koestler's image in *The Lion and the Ostrich*) had its head deep underground, but one advantage of being upside down and up to your neck in sand is that you are in no position to see how you look to others.

The self-satisfaction of political elites is frequently derided in the world of the arts. The question rarely asked is: if complacency is endemic across the spectrum of politics, and a British disease, might one not expect to find symptoms of a similar sickness in culture? Will not our new elites be as much inclined to overstate the flourishing of the arts as our politicians have traditionally tended to exaggerate the health of our finances or the stability of our institutions? And sure enough, their message has the same patrician overtones as that of Macmillan forty years ago: 'You've never had it so good.' Thatcher boasted that we had the world licked in economics. For the new elites we are the *fons et origo* of creativity. To rub the noses of lesser folk in their inadequacy, our foreign secretary, to my knowledge alone in the world, keeps a display of our achievements in design and manufacture in his swell Victorian office, like a window decor in a travel bureau. Victorian foreign secretaries, more secure in their ascendency, would have thought such self-advertisement horribly *infra dig*.

In culture the cascade of self-praise is never-ending. In music, pop and classical, in the novel, low, middle-brow and literary, in broadcasting, in theatre, in film, in architecture, in fashion and design – in every field you care to mention – representatives of culture and of authority, critics and cabinet ministers, combine to assure us that the Brits are top dogs. I am not aware of any country outside the former Soviet camp that preens itself on its performance in the arts in quite this way. (The French, not averse to a little cultural self-puffery, are in no position to boast at present.) Our arts elites appear to see themselves as New Elizabethans. It is easier to see them as Victorians in modern guise, whose impossible dream it is to combine the grandeur of the nineteenth century with the spirit of the sixties. As Britart shows, the result in culture can be at once strenuously novel and oddly stale.

The fact that the arts are indeed livelier than they were exacerbates the problem, by giving our claims to world supremacy a surface plausibility. Acting, architecture, fashion and design are fields where British achievements are recognized as outstanding in absolute terms. In others – notably the visual arts – the superiority we so loudly assert involves little intrinsic merit, depending as it does on mere modishness, the cult of celebrity and the paucity of the competition. Yet even if our assertions of overall excellence were justified – and in art, play-writing, music, film-making and literature they are clearly not – the volume of our auto-congratulation would be unseemly in a mature country. It is part of a general tendency by ministers and officials to resort to patriotic chuckings under the chin, as if they were boosting the confidence of a child, and at times the praise poured on to The People by the elites can outstrip the public's capacity to absorb it. When, in his millennium message to the nation, Tony Blair became carried away on the subject of 'the British genius' ('There's still no place on earth that has our combination of qualities. Our creativity, our determination, our courage, our sense of fairness . . .'), fair-minded listeners to the BBC queued up to telephone their indignation, courageously pointing out that foreigners were not without their little virtues or achievements. Such admirable level-headedness is enough to bring out the patriot in you.

Self-puffery in the arts, and the denigration of the foreigner it implies, have imperialistic echoes. The result can be a strange blimpishness in a place one would least expect to find it: on the centre-Left of politics and amongst the liberal intelligentsia, who once prided themselves on their internationalism. In the mouths of our cultural super-patriots 'our country, right or wrong' becomes 'our culture, good, poor or mediocre'. Sometimes the self-aggrandizement is little more than journalistic celebrity-mongering and cultural slumming: 'At no other time in its history has British art been so energetic, vibrant and above all fashionable,' wrote Rachel Campbell-Johnston in *The Times* of 4 August 1999 after a jolly outing with artists. (As with Bloomsbury art, Britart is highly *social*.) Sometimes it is governmental guff: 'I am also seeking to chart some of the astonishing progress that British creators are making at present,' said Chris Smith in his *Creative Britain*, oblivious of the Philistinism of the notion of 'progress' in the arts, let alone of governments charting it. And sometimes it teeters on the farcical. When William Hague boasted in a speech (26 January 1999) on *Identity and the British Way* 'We are the only country that could have come up with the Ministry of Silly Walks', he sounded like a character in *Ubu Roi* by Alfred Jarry, a foreigner with a gift for surreal humour of whom Mr Hague may or may not have heard. (*Fawlty Towers* would have been a more telling example of English comic invention, but for myth-making politicians the series had the drawback of being uncomfortably close to the truth.)

Our claims to ascendency in every field of the arts have their egalitarian, as well as patriotic logic. Once it was possible to acknowledge that our national performance in the visual arts, literature, music, the theatre or film was uneven in its quality, or underwent periods that were less fruitful than others. Today statements of the seemingly obvious – that the English genius tends to express itself most persuasively in poetry and fiction rather than painting or music – fall foul of several laws simultaneously: the law of continuous creativity, the law of the equal value of genres, the doctrine of national supremacy in all fields of the arts and the populist imperative. In an ultra-democracy all branches of the arts must be simultaneously in flower, not just in the metropolis but throughout the land. And should any depressions or protuberances of talent linger, the redistribution of funds from London to the regions, or from one genre to another, will even things up.

Obviously there can be high standards. There is a staple of fine performances in theatres, by orchestras or opera houses, and flashes of talent in the popular arts. It is the talk of an upsurge of creativity and originality that seems to me grossly inflated. No one has ever built a renaissance on performances of the classics, however innovative, on one or two architects, however gifted (and the irony is that we see so few of their best works in this country, e.g. by Will Alsop), still less on a clutch of over-exposed celebrities. Even our legendary proficiency at acting, though incontrovertible, can be double-edged. The fact that the British frequently provide the players has encouraged them to mistake the players for the play.

Defensive self-assertion characterizes culture in the widest sense. It is enough for our restaurants to improve, which they have, from a low base, for it to be suggested that French cuisine stands exposed as a myth and that here too the Brits are on top. In sport the same John Bullery is evident, if not the improvement. All it takes is for the English football team to qualify for the quarter finals and world victory is at once predicted. What is interesting about these and other claims to instant supremacy is their all-or-nothing flavour. The English novel is either flourishing or it is finished. The balloon of Cool Britannia is airborne one moment, deflated the next. English art is either an oxymoron or a world-beater. And when our sportsmen are not the champs, they are total rubbish.

Other cultures, notably America, undergo periods of self-doubt, yet no other country (with the possible exception of the French) suffers from these alternate bouts of despair and elation, of epilepsy and paralysis. Why is it that the British, seen as level-headed to the point of tedium, oscillate so violently between delusions of grandeur and bitter self-abasement? One can only put this death or glory spirit down to post-imperial trauma, and the reluctance of the country to face the reality of its condition. When it comes to the state of the nation we either exalt ourselves above all others or write ourselves off as a people foredoomed to decline. Every extreme is permitted. The only thought that is inadmissible is that we are a nation of middling wealth, middling novels, middling TV, middling-to-good opera, orchestras and actors, few and middling films, middling-to-poor footballers and cricketers, good-to-middling government and with middling-to-fair prospects. It hardly needs a psychoanalyst to point out that, were we to look the truth in the face, the prospects could be brighter.

A tendency to lose a sense of perspective is understandable in a country which, after a period of apparently irreversible decline, is commonly acknowledged to have raised its game. No one would deny that in culture, as in the economy, there is a new confidence, or that London is a far more vibrant place than it was. Yet to hear politicians, the press or cultural critics in full

patriotic cry, hailing yet another renaissance of British this or
English that, can be a disturbing experience, as if a person of
mature years had suddenly started behaving like an adolescent.
A curious psychological dualism appears to be at work. Our
self-glorification contains echoes both of Victorian complacency
and of the frantic boosterism of upstart communities in the
American Midwest. On the one hand we remain serene in our
superiority. On the other, like nineteenth-century America, we
are a country in a hurry, a brash self-advertising place whose
persistent insecurities are revealed in the urgency of its need to
impress itself and others.

And so, briefly, to the Dome. The real reason for pitying those
who live under authoritarian regimes, it has been suggested, is
that they are condemned to a lifetime of enthusiasm. Nothing is
more wearisome to the spirit than the insistence by the state that
its citizenry celebrate themselves and their achievements, and the
reluctance of the British to obey the injunction of sundry grinning
ministers, journalists and officials to celebrate to order may help
to account for their (to date) ambivalent attitude towards the
Dome. The view that the Dome lacks a purpose is not one I share,
since it seems to me a godsent illustration of the thesis of this
book. The psychology that led to its construction could hardly
be more revealing of our ruling caste's state of mind. Priggish,
hollow, self-aggrandizing, vapidly jokey, mincingly patriotic,
cynically populist, massively patronizing, mediocre to its soul
and curiously provincial – the Great White Wen of Greenwich
is a monument to the new elites erected by themselves.

'What does it mean to be British in the Year 2000?' The
question, inscribed above the entrance to the Dome's 'self-
portrait' zone, seems an invitation to yet another round of
self-applause. Yet it also suggests some uncertainty. And sure
enough the answer our ruling castes provide is as perplexing as
the question: 'It means being part of a nation that is at once
creative, honourable, brave, and yet able to laugh at itself.' Aside

from the faintly authoritarian echoes ('Long live the creative achievements of Soviet Man!' was a standard communist slogan), there are other problems. The political, cultural and business elites who together devised the Dome have taken it into their heads to shower praise on us. How are we, the brave, the creative British people, honourably to respond? Do we lower our eyes and stammer, 'Oh really, you shouldn't'? Do we cast off self-doubt, clasp hands and stride towards the future with firmer steps and uplifted gaze? Or, as a nation uniquely able to make fun of itself, do we dismiss this pitiful piece of marsh-mallow nationalism with a great peal of our unique, self-mocking laughter?

What officialdom clearly intended as a tribute to the health of the national psyche has the opposite effect. The bit about laughing at ourselves is especially worrying. A nation genuinely at ease would not need to bolster its self-image by boasting *to itself* of its penchant for self-deprecation. Nor do genuinely self-deprecating people simultaneously trumpet their virtues – their bravery, their creativity and the rest – unless, of course, they are schizophrenic, or otherwise troubled in their minds. And a country of brave, creative people which pours mockery on itself would indeed suggest a disturbed psyche. So one of two things must be true: either we are overstating our virtues or our self-mockery is in some degree false.

That single inscription in the Dome – cloying, banal, stupid as only high authority can be, and excruciatingly *de haut en bas* – sums up everything about the project. The patronizing essence of the Dome is the most significant thing about it. For a people to be patronized by its elites, even when they are distinguished statesmen, generals or cultural figures, is distasteful enough. To be patronized by new elite mediocrities is an affront to an entire society. Nothing could symbolize the fraudulence of our egalitarian oligarchs better than the spectacle of Lord Falconer, Minister for the Dome, friend of Tony Blair and a well-to-do lawyer whose children attend private schools, insisting to his fellow unelected peers in the gilt and red Upper Chamber that large numbers of the populace were having a most entertaining and instructive time at the millennial Dome.

From its beginnings the Dome was a top–down affair, a populist extravaganza foisted on a sceptical public from above. The flavour is New Labour but politically it was a cross-party initiative, and had the Tories continued in office it is unlikely that its fate or contents would have been much different. Implicit in its conception and execution was a kind of perky, Boy Scout nationalism that transcends conventional politics and is designed to appeal to what Dr Johnson once unkindly called 'plebeian patriotism'. Sceptics were duly branded as lacking an ambitious national spirit; as in the past, when in trouble, elites always have the patriotic card at the ready.

Two examples deserve to be recorded. In a letter to Tony Blair encouraging him to go ahead with the project after he came to office, Simon Jenkins, the *Times* columnist, a leading member of the Millennium Commission and an indefatigable promotor of the Dome, wrote: 'Greenwich will be the world's one big Millennium celebration . . . German, French, Italian and American planners all concede Britain's leadership here . . . Such events are milestones in a nation's history . . .'

The notion of foreigners 'conceding our leadership', question-able at the time (if there was ever a race to see who could spend most on the Millennium we were the only ones in it), becomes risible in retrospect, with the appointment of a Disney-trained Frenchman to rescue it from disaster. The second example is remarks made by Peter Mandelson, also a leading Dome pro-ponent, and for a time the minister responsible: 'There are too many in Britain who have forgotten what it is to be great as a country. Too many people have lost their ambition. Too many people just think that, well, we'll take second place to others who are better at doing these things . . . It's just a mentality. Lack of confidence. Lack of a sense of bigness or greatness by some people in Britain. I think it's pathetic. I hate it.'

Echoes of the old elites are unmistakable. There is nothing wrong with national ambition, or with thinking big. But to chide people for lacking a sense of greatness when they decline to exalt banality is a perverted form of patriotism. To anyone who has visited this 'milestone in a nation's history', seen the paltry exhibits, read the priggish slogans and shuddered at the crassness of the entire demeaning enterprise, the self-deception of those involved in its planning and promotion is breathtaking. How can they not have *known*? My guess is that they did, but so what? As Mandelson was quoted as saying, 'You have to remember that most people lead very humdrum lives.' The odour of cynicism inherent in any populist enterprise – 'never mind if the aim is low, *they* will enjoy this, this will be nice for *them*' – pollutes the Greenwich air. How can such mediocrity of aspiration be reconciled with Jenkins's assurance about foreigners conceding our leadership, or with the high ambitions for the nation proclaimed by Mandelson? To that there seems no answer, except to note that flauntingly patriotic elites, new or old, frequently turn out to have remarkably low expectations of their countrymen. For in the end they are not rejoicing in their nation, or its people. They are rejoicing in themselves.

The self-deception emerges clearly from the Dome's official history, written up by Adam Nicolson in a portentously entitled book, *Regeneration*. The conclusion reads:

The vision of the potent individual, embedded in the community of which he is part, which is familiar enough in the liberal American understanding of the relationship between self and society, has not until now been much of a presence in Britain. If the Dome manages, in some way, to liberate us into that new, ardent but humane vision of ourselves, then that will be a great legacy and the whole venture will have been more than worthwhile.

Nicolson's aspiration is right, yet the ethos of the Dome works in the opposite direction. It has nothing to do with the liberation of the individual, American-style. On the contrary, it is impossible to imagine a more elitist exercise, in the worst sense of the word. The Dome is the supreme example of our culture of condescension, in which the masses are tossed fragments of entertainment and instruction from on high, encouraged to content themselves with the meretricious and the second-rate, assured that it is the best in the world and told to 'celebrate' themselves, their country and their good fortune.

Authority is currently suggesting that the Dome was really for children – a revealing shift of emphasis. Its lack of mature content contrasts with the high seriousness and popular success of state-sponsored events in the past, whether the Great Exhibition of 1851, whose industrial wonders enthralled its visitors and filled them with legitimate national pride, or the *Exposition Universelle* in Paris in 1867, of which Flaubert wrote:

I have been twice to the exhibition. It's overwhelming. There are some splendid things . . . One would have to be familiar with all the Sciences and all the Arts to find interest in everything on view in the Champs de Mars. Still, someone who had three months to spare and went every day and took notes could save himself no end of reading and travel.

No one has said that of the Dome. As it happened, it coincided with the opening of the New York Planetarium (the Rose Centre for Earth and Space), a genuinely futuristic building housing a genuinely exciting exhibition with a high scientific and intellectual content. The signs are that it will be a popular success.

The symbolism of the Dome is so great it is hard to absorb at a go. What was meant to be a celebration of our creativity and sense of national purpose turned into its opposite: a colossal failure of imagination and an exhibition of aimlessness. What was designed to show that Britain was turned definitively towards the future merely illustrated how far our ruling castes, for all their modernist affectations, are nostalgic for the glory days of the past, while lacking the credentials of glory. What was intended to be a showcase of the democratic virtues has become a symbol of a sickly, demagogic society.

At the time of writing, the fate of the Dome is in the balance. If the people decline to respond in the hoped-for numbers to the summons to celebrate everything that is most banal and unaspiring in themselves, that would be a reason for genuine celebration.

The Tate Modern is a great improvement on the Dome, though here too patriotic braggadocio is the norm, notably in the press: 'British creators have smashed their tough witty past out of the twentieth century and looked brazen-faced towards a yet unmapped future,' said a *Times* leader on the opening. In fact there is little new at the Tate Modern. A national gallery of modern art was grossly overdue, though better late than never. Bankside, a fine old power station handsomely converted by Swiss architects, is a long way from the futuristic Bilbao. A twentieth-century building that harks back to nineteenth-century industrial grandeur, its main asset is its size. That is what everyone remarks on. As for the art, the most innovative work is by foreign artists born well over a century ago, but because of the Tate's conservatism in the past, its collection has large gaps. As more open-minded critics have noted, contemporary British work looks derivative and meretricious alongside the modern masters.

If these plain truths appear perverse, or an affront to the nation's virility, that is a measure of how far, in our curiously statist, officially euphoric culture, we have lost touch with cold objective fact.

6

Pop Politics

Nor is it by flattering [the crowd] with the most humiliating servility, as is done today, that one succeeds in seducing them. They back those who flatter them, but they back them with a just contempt, and as the flatteries become more excessive, they raise the level of their demands.

Gustave Le Bon, *Psychologie du Socialisme*

Democracy is not a church, the people are not divine and a wise electorate does not select its representatives for their ability reverently to echo the people's voice. The function of political leaders is to heed that voice but to speak with their own, in the common interest. This may involve saying things the public are reluctant to hear, but of whose veracity (assuming the leaders are speaking the truth as they see it) they are open to persuasion.

So it is that a true democracy should function. In the democracy we have, the leaders of society affect the accents of the people, literally in some cases. In so doing they are playing up to the myth of direct democracy: that leaders are the mouthpieces of the people and that the public are their ventriloquists. In practice it is the other way round. In ultra-democracies it is the leaders who are the ventriloquists, in whose mouths the voice of the people turns to caricature. And when they are misguided enough to echo their populist masters, it is the masses who end up as the dummies.

Rousseau saw direct democracy as impractical. Government

was too complex, the idea of minute by minute participation by the electorate unreal. Decisions would have to be taken in the name of the collective, in effect by political elites whose claim it was to reflect the so-called General Will. If direct democracy was seen as impossible in the eighteenth century, how much more today, when the sinuosities of government have increased a thousandfold? It is enough to think of the day-to-day administration of the social security system, or the shifting fortunes of the pound. Even allowing for improvements in education, for millions of perfectly intelligent people the Medium Term Financial Strategy is little more than a voodoo incantation. Unless they devote their minds to it and to little else, the organization of modern society is quite simply too intricate for individuals to comprehend.

It was this that led Michels to his 'iron law of oligarchy':

It is organization which gives birth to the domination of the elected over the electors, of the mandatories over the mandators, of the delegates over the delegators. Who says organization says oligarchy . . . The most formidable argument against the sovereignty of the masses is . . . derived from the mechanical and technical impossibility of its realization. (*Political Parties*)

This was written before universal suffrage, and decades before the mass consumer society. The more complex the organization, the greater the need for it to be competently managed. It follows, perversely, that a highly evolved democracy with a neo-liberal economic system emphasizing individual choice will produce oligarchies of matching power. In other words, the more prosperous and democratized a society becomes, the greater its reliance on elites. It is not a happy message, so it is not the one the public are given. The dream of direct democracy remains alluring and our populist oligarchies think it wise to connive in the illusion. Everywhere contacts between voters and the elected appear to be intensifying, narrowing the gap between the rulers and the ruled. Opinion polls, vox pop, focus groups, the Internet, the growing influence of the media – the people would seem to be involved in their governance as never before. The new elites claim that all this brings us closer to the democratic dream. Democrats in the true sense will wish to examine the nature and quality of the dialogue between government and the governed more critically.

Before taking the argument further, the author would like to avail himself of this opportunity to reaffirm his belief in the common man, if only because we all fall within that capacious category, and (divinities apart) there is no one else to believe in. The purpose of this book, however, is not to enunciate pieties, but to demonstrate how those who will hear no wrong of the people are usually the first to abuse their trust. To suggest, as I shall do, that our political arrangements, despite progress, and although I have seen far worse abroad, retain imperfections, and that the common man is not without his faults, is not to suggest that democracy should be abandoned as a failure. The following paragraphs should be read with this in mind.

Contact between politicians and the people is an excellent thing. In principle. In reality the contact can be as phoney as the advantages can be overstated. Once politicians could be dangerously aloof from the public; today the danger is of a spurious proximity. To gain an image of ultra-democracy in action one must imagine politicians making round-the-clock speeches whose script is electronically revised in accordance with the readings of a clapometer: if the audience do not react well to a paragraph the succeeding one will be automatically adjusted to reflect their response. Seen this way, democracy becomes a sort of referendum in slow motion, one whose results are never final as governments, reacting to instant opinion and the latest headcount, constantly modify the question to elicit a more positive reaction. (If the analogy sounds far-fetched, remember that Hollywood studios now show films to specimen audiences before release: should they prefer a happy to a tear-jerking ending, the scriptwriters can oblige.)

Politicians today find themselves submerged in a perpetual *bain de foule*, a crowd-bath whose waters turn from warm to chilly in an instant. Partly it is because of new technologies of communication. These have an intrinsically populist element, in as much as they enhance the tyranny of numbers. Everywhere its pressure is felt. 'The weight of opinion', the 'overwhelming view', 'a crushing majority'. What if it is wisdom and reflection that are crushed, overwhelmed, weighted down by sheer numbers? What if that which is gained in speed and directness of response is lost in rationality? And, most dangerous of all, what if politicians become so skilled in their ventriloquism that they are able to communicate thoughts to the public the public never knew it had?

The Internet is an example of the dubious merits of intensified communication in populist hands. Of what advantage is it to democracy that from 1998 the Prime Minister could pretend to converse directly with individuals, when in reality all that is happening is that the public's all too predictable complaints are computed by party officials and a pro-forma reply, purporting to come from the PM's mouth, is keyed into the machine? One can see the benefits to the Government, but not to the public. In this and other ways direct democracy in its modern guise becomes simultaneously reality and myth. Also, much instant information comes in the form of pictorial imagery, where mass communication is cankered by mass emotion. The impulses passing to and fro between the elector, the media and the elected may now be transmitted at unprecedented speeds and frequency, but the communication of irrationality, demagogy and sheer falsehood have never been faster either. After seeing on their sitting-room screens the picture of the little girl who has been raped and murdered, and the mugshot of the paedophile who has committed the crime, most people do not want to hear about how he himself was abused as a child, they want him hanged.

The phenomenal increase of letters, faxes or phone calls to MPs' offices would also appear to be a democratic plus. Again, things are less simple. In reality the subjects on which MPs are approached often lie outside their province, and the letters not infrequently convey extreme or dotty views which do not merit the cost of the return fax, phone call or stamp. The apocryphal response to such importunings – a printed card from the MP saying 'I am sorry to tell you that your letter has not been selected for reply' – is today a parliamentary joke; not long ago it was close to the reality. Seasoned MPs are amazed by the growth of such correspondence over the last twenty years. It says much for the grievance culture that letters to MPs are the one area where letter-writing has not gone into decline.

Face-to-face contacts are far more frequent too (though not public meetings, which have suffered from the competition of television). Retired politicians recall the time when they scarcely went to their constituencies. Should they decide that electoral considerations made it advisable to call by, their presence was seen as a gracious gesture, like a sovereign visiting a far-flung colony. In the course of this royal progress the MP would open something or other, preferably a school or home for the elderly bearing his or her name, converse with local dignitaries, be photographed chatting to a few constituents, attend a local party function and be gone. Today MPs are expected to have a home in their constituency, and the majority go there most weekends, whether they have a small or large majority, and whether or not there is anything much for them to do. Amongst the over-zealous, absenteeism has become presenteeism, its equal and opposite vice.

Surgeries are held far more often than in the past, in busy or deprived constituencies once a week. Sometimes the purpose is to help people in genuine distress solve their problems, sometimes to put on a show of availability, as a means of self-publicity. And, of course, the greater the availability the higher the demand. The proliferation of surgeries encourages a culture of complaint, in the way that children are liable to develop anxieties when they sense that their parents are anxious for their welfare. What many visitors are after is therapy, a soothing illusion that the state can provide cures for their ills, and increasingly that is all they get. Frequently they are people who, being neither poor nor sick, are capable of looking after themselves. But on the whole, they would rather not. The French philosopher Jean Baudrillard has described this tendency with his usual dark humour in *Le Paroxyste Indifférent*:

The state goes on liberating its citizens, encouraging them to take care of themselves, which they generally do not want at all. In that sense we are all Bartlebys. 'Be free! Be responsible! Take yourself in hand!' implores the state. 'I would prefer not to.' People would prefer not to run, not to compete, not to consume, not to be free at any price . . . They are almost astonished to have children. They are astonished to have to take charge of themselves. They haven't got the conviction for it, they are persuaded of nothing. They are even astonished to have a body.

(As a former MP I can vouch for the truth of this last sentence. It is amazing how many people see their bodies as an arbitrary encumbrance for which they have no personal responsibility. In an ideal world they would be happy to surrender them, like delinquent children, to the safe-keeping of the authorities.)

Again Tocqueville foresaw it all, when he talked of how democracy could give rise to a new form of servitude, 'well-organized, soft and peaceable', in which the individual's will would be numbed by democratic power:

It doesn't break people's wills, it softens, bends and directs them. It doesn't often force people to act, but it constantly opposes action. It doesn't destroy things, it prevents them coming into the world. It does not tyrannize, it obstructs, it constricts, it enervates, it extinguishes, it deadens, and finally it reduces each nation to being no more than a herd of timid, industrious animals, of which the government is the keeper.

It is distressingly easy to gain a reputation for being 'a good constituency MP'. People do not necessarily mean that he or she has done anything for them that they could not have achieved through more regular channels, such as the local authorities, or that the MP has succeeded in transforming the economic fortunes of his or her patch. What they mean is that they have been seen about the place and have put on a convincing face of solicitude about problems they may be in no position to resolve, and which may or may not fall within their field of responsibility in the first place. At best the MPs will become adept at selecting the deserving causes, act on them energetically and disregard the rest. At worst they will find themselves becoming something between a curate and an insurance salesman: a listening figure who communes with human souls in their real or imaginary distress, and a glib talker selling panaceas for all problems on the never-never.

Like it or not (it may be objected), this is the way modern democracies work. The truth is that remarkably few people, whether MPs or constituents, know how our democracy works. Parliamentary procedures are so complex or mildewed with age that they are frequently not understood by MPs themselves. As for the voters, an astonishing number have failed (or are unwilling) to grasp one of democracy's basic principles: that a representative is not a delegate, and that it is not the job of MPs to do what the voters want. Their task is to listen to what the elector says and make up their minds on the basis of the facts, their estimate of the voters' best interests and their personal convictions, while taking into account the greater scheme of things. At the next election the voters will have a chance to vent their feelings about whether or not the MPs turn out to have done the right thing, and to measure his or her promises against the results.

If the pressures on political elites have never been greater, they are in no position to complain; often it is they who, desperate to display themselves as faithful executors of the people's will, engender those pressures by promising that which cannot be delivered. The NHS is the most current and most flagrant example. The debates that follow the annual crises concentrate on the quantity of government funding, yet that is not the basic issue. The point is that no analogous country promises to supply free medical care (prescriptions excepted but hospital hotel costs included) to all its citizens from taxation, irrespective of their wealth, regardless of the expense of new technology and without reference to the geometrically rising demands of an ageing population. The result of this wholly unrealistic undertaking is that, though funding has been constantly increased under all governments, and despite the best efforts of its overworked staff, the NHS, traditionally a source of national pride, provides a worse service than those of most Western countries. So why the pride?

The NHS is a classic example of the demagogy of political elites, and the repercussions on the public. Their heads softened by years of competitive ingratiation, the public have become sentimentally attached to an unworkable system, and will contemplate no other. Rich or poor, they would prefer everything free, and to promise them the unattainable has become a gauge of a caring politician. No party can face up to the need for limitations on what can be provided, or for new sources of finances, for fear of being accused by opponents of reneging on this sacramental commitment. The endlessly reiterated vow to observe the people's wish for a totally free NHS funded by taxation is a form of political cynicism in which all parties collude. Meanwhile the service becomes increasingly unreliable, but only those with sufficient means can go private. So it is the average man who in the end suffers from the delusions sown in his mind by the elites. The parallels with education need no underlining.

It is in the nature of ultra-democracies to undertake to provide more than they can deliver. Consequently they deliver less than they should to the truly needy. Like high-street banks who promise a personalized service for every client, they end up fobbing their customers off with generalized information ('Dear

Barclaycard Holder') or maddening recorded messages. The bulk of the exchanges between MPs and their electors are increasingly formulaic, with the flavour of adverts, mail-shots or commercial circulars. The constituent, inflamed by some tendentious or inaccurate press report (the details of the matter are normally too complex to be ingested by the press, let alone the individual), volunteers or is goaded into appending her signature to a stock letter of complaint, concocted by some pressure group or single-issue lobby. In return she will receive a stock response ('Dear Constituent'), thoughtfully supplied to the MP by the government.

Single issue lobbies, for the disabled, the aid budget, education or the arts, see themselves as the *ne plus ultra* of democracy. In fact they are part of a false dialogue between government and electors. Thriving as they do on moralism, sentimentalism and financial irresponsibility, such lobbyists are guaranteed a flourishing future in populist democracies. They are moralistic rather than moral because they decline to take account of the effect of their demands on others. They are sentimentalists because they trade on instant feeling, e.g. for the disabled. And they are financially irresponsible because each lobby casts aside all economic rationality in favour of the cause – though if asked for their views, those campaigning for more money for the arts would also pronounce themselves in favour of more for foreign aid and more for the disabled. It does not occur to them that they are behaving immorally, in the sense that there can be no morality without practicality. Yet another field where populist politics are fundamentally unethical.

The rise of 'community politics' reflects a similar trend. 'Communal action' rarely signifies doing something in common: more often it means little more than agitating for a common advantage – not the same thing at all. Stripped of its sanctimonious, ultra-democratic overtones, communitarian politics can be no more than self-interested groups of individuals forming up to government to secure more benefits for themselves, and to hell with the rest. Seen as the most advanced expression of democracy, in reality community action frequently comes down to a kind of organized egotism. And needless to say, it tends to be the more prosperous communities, with their superior organization and articulate, well-placed spokesmen, who come off best.

A noisy concern for democratic involvement and dedication to the public weal can thus come to mean their very opposite: a clamour by each interest group for a bigger slice of the pie, which must of necessity be at the expense of others. Far from being an exercise in fairness or redistribution, community or single issue politics can easily degenerate into a Hobbesian war for advantage of all against all. A war conducted by ultra-democratic means, in which everything, it goes without saying, is done in the sacred name of equality.

The struggle for sectional advantage in drawing on the common purse is accepted as a fact of life, and no one troubles to point out its internal contradictions. The elderly demand higher pensions, the young more for education. The jobless want more generous benefits, the employed want tax cuts. Athletes and sportsmen insist on subsidies which can only come from the same communal purse that gives help to invalids. Discussion of policy options – who should get what – is conducted increasingly through the media, and it is there that one can listen in to a nation's conversation with itself. Passing judgement on the tone of the national debate may seem a breach of democratic propriety, yet if we do not hesitate to characterize the style of other countries (in France the public debate is said to be dominated by technocratic elites, in America by far-out populists like Rush Limbaugh), why not our own?

The confidence with which the average citizen enunciates his or her views on radio or TV has grown enormously. Thirty years ago, had they been offered a platform at all, many would have clammed up, dumbstruck, at the sight of a microphone or a camera. Now all add their voices to the chorus of opinion without hesitation. Surely another advance for democracy? Indubitably, though the result is often far from the informed exchange of opinion one might ideally like to see. Sometimes the vox pop is intelligent and articulate, sometimes articulate but unintelligent, more often intelligent but inarticulate. Sometimes people contribute enlightening views from direct experience. Frequently they give voice to harmless verities. Occasionally they are nuts. Most often, however, the views they enunciate with a sort of peeved self-righteousness are banalities, and whatever the subject, invariably such voices are tinged with complaint. *I think the state should do more . . . We need more resources . . . The government is out of touch . . .*

In individual cases, they may be right. In general, it is an incontestable truth that the chorus of complaint is swelling ever louder at a moment when the state is spending more than ever in history, when government is involved in our individual lives to an unprecedented degree and when, as we have seen, political elites of whatever complexion have never been more assiduous in seeking to ascertain what the people think.

What is remarkable about the overall tone of public debate in Britain is no longer its deference to authority in the old, hierarchical sense, but its opposite: the deference that mass opinion affords to itself. Ours is supposedly a society that treasures the liberty and distinctiveness of the individual, yet increasingly we converse in borrowed tongues: borrowed from the discourse of the day, borrowed from the media, borrowed from each other. As freedom of popular expression grows, the Johnsonian tradition of sturdy individualism and rational dissent is less and less in evidence. Even allowing for the fact that those who offer their opinions may be unrepresentative, it is rare to find members of the public who will give an honest-to-God, commonsense view couched in their own words and based on first-hand experience on current problems. More often they parrot the pieties of the day, in all their simple-mindedness and soupy squalor.

Where did mass man – which is to say the average man, be he manual labourer or hereditary peer – learn such distressing habits of thought? Is it possible that, unconsciously, he is echoing the stances and rhetoric of the political class he insists that he despises? If so, we should not be surprised. Mass societies massify opinion. The result in politics can be a form of crowd dynamics, in which the elites and the mass can suck one another down, in a vortex-like motion. Meanwhile the voice of the commonsense individual is swamped, or distorted beyond recognition.

The 'spinning' of government messages is an example of this *de facto* collusion between electors and elected. Once governments confined themselves to manipulating the presentation of the news behind the public's back. Now they do it openly, flaunting their skills, and the more successful the spinners show themselves at moulding (or misleading) opinion, the greater their popular renown. Like the barrow boys in Petticoat Lane who convert their sales patter into entertainment, the spin doctors become performers, artists in persuading the people to buy their bull. In this way the public end up conniving in their own fooling, while transforming those whose job it is to delude them into celebrities.

There is no mystery about how the moulding of mass opinion works. As every politician knows, it is easier to dominate a large crowd than a small audience. Large groups, swayed by the emotions of togetherness, react collectively. Small groups, even if composed of the same people, are more individual, more questioning. On the BBC's *Any Questions* it is enough for any speaker to make the usual pan-humanitarian noises in favour of more government action or spending on whatever is the cause of the day for the audience to erupt in acclamation; warm feelings are contagious, and when his conscience is stoked to a fury man in the mass spontaneously ignites. This does not mean that he or she is irredeemably blockheaded. If the same sentiments were expressed to an audience of twenty or thirty people drawn from the same gathering, many would pull sceptical faces, and there would be mutterings of 'That's all very well, but how is it going to be paid for?' As Aldous Huxley reflected, 'The quality of moral behaviour varies in inverse ratio to the number of human beings involved.'

The contagion of received opinion is reminiscent of the course of the photographic revolution (to which, through the homogenizing effects of TV, it is indirectly linked). In early portraits the impression of truth is overwhelming. The subjects, dressed in their everyday clothes and facing a medium to which they were not yet accustomed, remained ingenuously themselves: somewhat puzzled, a little po-faced perhaps, but with no attempt to pose. The impression was one of unmediated veracity, which is why old photographs have the impact they do. Later, our knowingness increased. Confronted with a camera we began to adopt a self-conscious (often smiley) demeanour, and to play up to our own or other people's image of ourselves. Today's electronic media evoke a similar, conventionalizing response, as we tend to strike poses and to say what is expected. The camera, it could almost be said, encourages us to lie.

The homogenization of sentiment induced by the media makes reasoned dissent difficult. Fear of affronting mass opinion deforms democratic debate, the more so in a society where mass man continues to be confused with the poor, the uneducated or the deprived. Questioning the wisdom of massified opinion is seen as elitist in itself. In such an atmosphere, dissent from the conventional view can easily become self-conscious, evasive and insincere, the dissenters more concerned with striking counter-suggestive attitudes than with confronting problems. When columnists or opinion-formers go flamboyantly against the grain it is often little more than affectation: the dandyism of the professional controversialist whose paradoxes are designed to startle rather than to inform, and whose stagily non-conformist views are as much proof of heterodox thinking and true conviction as the wearing of different coloured socks.

Nothing is more predictable than the willed eccentric, and

not a few of our most celebrated 'mavericks' are automata of contradiction. People say one thing, I shall say differently. Families falling apart? Good thing too! Too few students studying maths and science? Excellent! Increased crime? Figment of the imagination! To stand conventional opinion on its head is simply another way of thinking conventionally. Inverted elites in the media come in two varieties: those who pander to populist taste and those who preen themselves on their dissent. The former seek to flatter the masses, the latter to awe them by a false display of heterodox thinking. Either way, the ultimate purpose is to set themselves above them.

In politics the culture of pretence flourishes. In our managerial era politicians are obliged to simulate conflict in much the same way that our contemporary artists or pop musicians simulate protest. All parties would indignantly reject this view, but their agonized denials, like their agonistic rituals in Parliament, are largely for the form. To anyone not caught up in the game, the combat between Left and Right looks increasingly like a re-staging of Civil War battles by Cromwellian enthusiasts: colourful pennants, charging horses, loud explosions, no one killed.

In a rational world the decline of old-style politics would lessen the need for elites to insinuate themselves into the affections of the masses. Yet far from diminishing, populism is forever seeking new outlets. The less meaningful the differences between politicians, the more strident their voices grow, to catch the ear of a bored and inattentive public. Political parties have to compete about something. It used to be for the hearts and minds of the people, now it is just their hearts. So it is that rivalry has shifted from programmes to personalities, from economic and social creeds to varieties of populist styles.

To be a good politician it has never been necessary to be an intellectual – rather the contrary – but till now neither has it been thought necessary to incline the knee too abjectly before the masses. James Callaghan and Margaret Thatcher were not especially cultivated, in the intellectual or artistic sense, yet neither did they go out of their way to abase themselves before popular taste. Now the aim appears to be that nothing should be above the heads of a single voter. John Major was plain-spoken to the point of inarticulacy. Blair goes one further by democratizing his accent and indulging in vaporous chat. Major admitted to reading the novels of Jeffrey Archer, not for effect, which would have been forgivable, but by choice and for plea-sure, which is not. Blair trumped him again by inviting DJs and the like to Number 10. Major advertised his passion for cricket. Blair prefers the more popular football.

Meanwhile, flattery of the masses by political elites has reached Tartuffian proportions. As we have seen, Tony Blair never tires of telling us how creative we are, which is nice for us. Last year Lady Thatcher, who has put aside decent reserve out of office, assured a Conservative conference that 'We are the best in Europe.' Nice for us too. But it was William Hague who was nicest of all. In the course of a single speech he described the British as ambitious, sporty, fashion-conscious, self-confident, international, tolerant, distinctive, loyal, brassy, reserved, polite, independent, not class-ridden, open, mobile, charitable, enterprising, law-abiding, multi-ethnic, inclusive, forward-looking, courageous, mature, youthful and as having a fine sense of humour. His audience would have needed it to sit through the speech.

It is a strange sort of democracy where the more we spend on education, the lower the tone of democratic debate. All this is happening at a time when our universities are turning out three times more graduates than two decades ago. Logically our leaders should be raising the stakes, peppering their speeches with scientific formulae and literary quotations, rather than mouthing demotic tags. The same process which has produced our inverted political elites appears to have given rise to an inverse law of democracy: that the more educated a people becomes, the more its leaders talk down to them. Either there is something wrong with the leaders, or with the education. Some may say both.

The Budget ceremony illustrates how the new elites continue to play the old patrician game in modern guise. Unlike other countries, Britain has always made a spectacle of its Budget: the Chancellor's walk in the park, the teasing hints, the dangling in the face of the public of the worn red box like a Christmas gift ('Guess what daddy has got in here for you?') Now that the government no longer sets interest rates or controls nationalized industries, and the global market pre-determines so much of our economic policies, one might have thought that New Labour would have modernized the ritual, just as it is modernizing the House of Lords. Yet nothing changes. With its little trumperies and trickeries, as money is transferred from one pocket to another and cherries are tossed to the public to keep them sweet, the Budget ceremonial continues to be what it has always been: a way of keeping the masses in a state of economic dependency by populist means.

Anxiety to ingratiate themselves with the electorate is written on official faces. It has been insufficiently remarked on that, before the last few years, political leaders did not spend their every waking hour smiling. Neither Callaghan nor Thatcher were smilers – rather the reverse – nor did Macmillan or Churchill seek to irradiate the lives of the people with a sunny grin. Prime ministers and leaders of the opposition smile now, constantly, their features forever frozen in a fixed, indiscriminate rictus of insinuation. Even on state occasions they exude a vacant humour of the kind that Wyndham Lewis, a genuinely humorous man, once satirized in his futurist magazine *Blast*:

BLAST HUMOUR
Quack ENGLISH drug for stupidity and sleepiness
Arch enemy of REAL, conventionalizing like
Gunshot, freezing supple
Real in ferocious chemistry of Laughter.

In most people's schooldays smirking at nothing was considered by teachers an irritating habit: 'Wipe that smile off your face, boy!' Now it is authority itself that stands grinning before the class, in the hope of attracting its admiration and affection; a minor but telling instance of the supplicating attitudes common amongst inverted elites.

If populist politics cannot provide genuine participation, at least it can provide the trappings. A simple way to create an illusion of extended democracy is to multiply the number of its representatives. Sagacious observers (including the most recent Sergeant at Arms) long ago concluded that there is a case for a smaller House of Commons, and a cut of a third has been suggested. Yet now, instead of fewer directly elected representatives, we are promised more.

Of the new bodies – the Scottish and Welsh Assemblies, the promised regional assemblies, an elected Mayor of London and the possibility of a semi-elected House of Lords – there is a case for Scotland and London, but none for the rest. If cynicism and apathy about politics are growing, how much greater will they be when the number of elected posts is more than doubled? Ever lower participation in elections could return to positions of authority an ever larger complement of people who have no business in public office: time-servers, careerists, political zealots, people whose level of intelligence would disgrace a town hall, cranks and incompetents of every sort. If a significant proportion of MPs are less inspiring than we would prefer, what can we expect from newly elected institutions whose candidates are likely to include a large element of rejected candidates for the Commons?

Elites look after their own, the new elites are no different, and one result of these 'extensions of democracy' will be a massively swollen political class. Inevitably it will develop its army of hangers-on: researchers, specialists in public relations, constituency agents and activists, lobbyists of every kind, many of them paid in one form or another from public funds. And what will be the role of the new politicians? To boost their reputation as caring citizens by promising to spend public money they will have no responsibility for raising and which the government has not got. Each and every candidate for each and every office will be fecund in ideas of how to improve our lives – if only they had the resources . . .

Imposing ever more tiers of government will not increase democracy, it will allow ultra-democracy to run amok. The low calibre of candidates for the post of mayor of London, a sophisticated metropolis, is an augury of what we can expect. If regional assemblies are pursued and the House of Lords is wholly or partially elected, a citizen living in a small British town would be the proud possessor of a total of seven votes: for a town council, a district council, a county council, a regional assembly, a European Parliament, the Westminster Parliament and the House of Lords. The reforms are billed as a decentralizing measure, yet the result could well be the reverse: the political parties will seek to bring the new institutions into their orbit by inserting their placemen, as we have seen in Scotland, in Wales and in London, and governments will naturally strive to curtail the extravagances and self-indulgence of local politicians whose funds are not locally raised. Watching these tiers of administration spiralling skywards, voters are unlikely to feel that they are being given a greater voice in their lives. There is nothing like an over-profusion of institutions of doubtful representativeness to give democracy a bad name. Cynicism about politicians seems all too likely to grow in proportion to their numbers.

Even before the new institutions are in place, indifference to politics is growing. Turnouts in elections are in vertiginous decline. In the 1997 election there was a drop of some 5 per cent. In the most recent local and European elections a mere quarter of the electorate troubled themselves to vote, and on the momentous occasion of the establishment of the new Scottish

Assembly, the first the Scottish people had enjoyed in 600 years, only 58 per cent of electors celebrated by performing their civic duty. The most striking aspect of this galloping apathy is how little it is discussed. Politicians and commentators continue to interpret election results in fine and exhaustive detail, as if nothing had changed. How a public consultation from which three-quarters of eligible voters have abstained can be seen as a valid exercise in establishing what the public think, no one explains. In a sense the political class have little option but to ignore the reality: for them and their shadows in the media to acknowledge that their game was in danger of becoming a minority sport would be an intolerable blow to the prestige and self-esteem on which the game depends.

For all the new techniques of persuasion employed by MPs and their parties, and their obsequious behaviour, the love-hate attitude of the public towards politicians shows signs of tilting in a less loving direction. A Sod's Law of democracy appears to be at work: that the more representative of the people the political elites strive to appear, and the more the people see of them, the more the status of politicians slips in the people's eyes.

The climate is ripe for the rise of a new type of populist, typified by Ken Livingstone, who portrays himself as standing outside the conventional order: an anti-politician, in a word, who assumes the posture of a radical. As in pop music and contemporary art, his radicalism is actually rather dated, old lamps buffed up as new. But mock-radical politics, like Murray Mint pop, clearly sells. In an economically successful society bored with conventional politics, people are attracted by the idea of striking radical postures without the risk entailed in radical belief. Livingstone is a virtual revolutionary who enjoys enormous virtual support. The aim is not to overthrow the existing order, or even to change it much, but to dance and buzz like a fly in the beam of public attention, without getting trapped in the drear business of day-to-day decision-making and administration, wherein no glory or celebrity lie.

New Labour has only itself to blame. It was the Blair government that took flattery of the public to new extremes, and Mandelson who contrived a blend between politics and the celebrity culture. It was they who made anti-elitism a leitmotiv, while seeking to impersonate the common man. In so doing they have helped set the stage that Livingstone, a more convincing mass man than themselves, now occupies. With few powers, and therefore few responsibilities to encumber him, Livingstone has taken populist politics to its logical conclusion. The lesson of his success seems unlikely to be lost on the next generation of political elites.

In the longer term, populist politics are doomed because their promises are a mirage. The public will always ask for more, and always it will be disappointed. As Nietzsche said in another context: 'They think they are leading the people but when they look round they find they are chasing them.' Ultra-democracy stimulates unreal expectations and anarchic demands, and governments are forever attempting to square the circle. The consequence is a paradox, of which we are seeing ever more examples: that excessive expectations of democracy lead to increased central control. Anthony Barnett, an imaginative political thinker, believes this leads to what he calls corporate populism, where the government finds itself behaving like a large company:

Corporate control is based on central strategic power – a focus on inputs and flexible management – while sales require market populism. Rich and poor alike should want to enjoy the corporation's products, whether plastics, supermarkets or television shows. Its public products should never be too low brow or too high brow. Rather, the aim should be a classless universal appeal. (*Prospect* magazine)

Corporate populism, he concludes, attends to our feelings but maintains our dependency. 'It is the modernization of subjecthood.'

And there is the key. As voter and consumer, mass man resembles an absolute monarch. Yet his power is illusory. However imperious the king's voice, in reality he reverts to the position of a subject, his tastes and desires manipulated by oligarchies who re-invent the relationship between the masses and the ruling caste in modern guise. However abjectly the new elites incline their heads before him, like so many courtiers, mass man, our king of kings, turns out to be no more than a pawn. At some point one must hope he will become aware of the indignity of his position.

7

Pop Media

It seems to me that in the whole of Europe the cultural elite is yielding to other elites. Over there [in communist countries] to the elite of the police apparatus. Here, to the elite of the mass media apparatus.

Milan Kundera, *The Art of the Novel*

In the 1974 general election, when Edward Heath confronted the coal miners and lost, the question he put to the electorate was *who governs Britain?* Today the answer of the man on the street would clearly not be 'the trade unions', yet nor might it be 'Parliament'. His reply, only half-sardonic, might often be 'the media'. The fourth estate, *arrivistes* of ultra-democracy, are leapfrogging the other three. As politics fall into decline, the media, from which commerce is inseparable, is emerging as the most powerful of the new elites. The three still work in harness, though there can be rivalry and shifting loyalties. What is certain is that the media is far less deferential to government than it was, a change most glaringly symbolized by its reluctance to hush up the sexual misdemeanours of politicians. The evolution of this triangular relationship – government, commerce and the media – over the last few decades is best expressed in parable form:

Once, Politics and Media were a couple. They made a fractious pair. Politics – a domineering figure, prematurely grave – was inclined to wax eloquent over dinner about the burdens of office, endlessly chiding Media for her light-mindedness. The trouble with you, he would sigh as he poured his first whisky and settled down to his red boxes of an evening, is that you have no idea of the meaning of the word responsibility.

And Politics had a point. Media was a wilful woman, younger than her husband, and led him something of a dance, forever teasing Politics about his self-importance or insisting that he was completely out of touch. Yet theirs was one of those relationships where things are not what they seem. In truth Politics and Media were a complementary couple, and for all her lippiness Media was secretly respectful of Politics' status and revelled in his confidences. Media liked nothing better than to be in the know and pass on gossip to her wide circle of acquaintances. With his third whisky inside him, or after some amorous bout, or both, Politics told her things of such exquisite sensitivity they sent tremors down her spine – though naturally on a background basis, not for use.

Such was Media's respect for Politics that, when she discovered that, the burdens of office notwithstanding, he had found time for affairs, rather than walk out on him, she bit her lip and kept quiet about it. So things continued for a number of years. Finally, feeling that her loyalty was being taken for granted, and that her attachment to Politics was thwarting her ambitions, Media decided to break free.

Naturally, there was a scene. She explained to Politics that she was tired of hushing up his affairs simply because he was a public figure, tired of her dependency and, as she put it, needed her own space. Suit yourself, said Politics, affecting equanimity, though privately he felt rejected. Not that he was entirely surprised by her behaviour. For some time there had been signs that Media was growing apart from him. She had even stopped showing interest in his red boxes and spreading her news. Once Media could never get enough of Politics. Now, even when he told her things that would have had her in fits of excitement,

Media scarcely troubled to pass them on, for the simple reason that no one wanted to know. She thinks me a dull fellow, past his prime, Politics had begun to suspect, and he was right. The truth was, Politics had begun to bore her.

In her late thirties now, Media threw herself into a crash programme of self-rejuvenation. Once, beneath the light-mindedness, she had been a serious woman. Now she gave herself over to every extravagance, spending the whole time chattering about fashion, food fads, pop stars, celebrities and sex. Politics worried about what Media might get up to in her new state of mind, and with good reason. Before long Media had embarked on a tempestuous affair. Her lover, Commerce, was a seductively irreverent fellow on whom this once proud woman became pathetically dependent. With him she felt young again, and for him she was ready to do things she had never done for Politics, debasing herself in all manner of ways, best left to the imagination.

Politics and Media had not formally parted, and Media still kept a pied à terre *in Politics' house, for mutual convenience, while spending most of her time with Commerce. Politics' relations with Commerce were edgy, as might be expected: Politics thought Commerce a vulgar fellow, while Commerce treated Politics as a figure of fun. A low point came when Media, egged on by Commerce, began bruiting it about that Politics had had mistresses, causing Politics no end of trouble. All those years of discretion and now this! For him the really mortifying part was that, though Media's affair with Commerce was common knowledge, far from crying scandal, no one seemed in the least bit interested. Dual standards, Politics thought bitterly.*

He was tempted to have it out with Commerce, but restrained himself: he knew him for a ruthless individual, capable of manip-ulating Media against him in all manner of ways, and if there was one thing Politics understood, it was the realities of power. The fact was that Media had thrown in her lot with Commerce because he was going up in the world while Politics was coming down. There was no hope of enticing her back, still less of her resuming her old, submissive ways. Politics was left with no choice but to swallow his pride and work out a modus vivendi *with Commerce.*

When they met to talk things over, somewhat to their surprise, Politics and Commerce hit it off. And how could they not? They had shared interests. They talked the same language. They discovered friends in common. In fact it turned out that Commerce's customers and Politics' voters were exactly the same people. In no time at all an accommodation was reached. Media was delighted, joking in her roguish way that if the deal meant that the rival couples were to become a threesome, she was all for it.

Their relationship – one of those modern, pragmatic arrangements – thrived. Politics and Commerce found little ways to be helpful to one another, as friends should, and when it came to sharing the affections of Media, a tacit understanding was reached. In an effort to keep up with Commerce and Media, Politics too set out to rejuvenate himself. Gone was his gravitas as he began dressing more snappily and, determined to keep up with Media's zestful style, lost no opportunity to show off his somewhat shaky familiarity with the culture of the times: pop stars, football scores, that kind of thing. When Media got a little out of hand, as she frequently did, and began baiting Politics cruelly about his new-found trendiness, it was enough for Politics to have a word with Commerce for him to rein her in.

As in the best threesomes, there were squabbles. Though even when tensions flared and Commerce threatened to turn Media against Politics if Politics did not show himself a little more attentive to Commerce's concerns, things were smoothly and expeditiously settled by the simple expedient of Politics backing down. The truth was that Politics, poor fellow, was very much the junior partner, while Commerce was top dog, with Media . . . well, Media was always somewhere in the middle.

When it began to be whispered that Media was a flighty woman, mindful of what was left of her reputation, she denied it. Though happy to spread tittle tattle about other people's lives, she had a way of coming over all puritanical the moment anything was said about her own. Saying she was in the habit of bedding down with Politics one day and with Commerce the next was a disgraceful slur. She was an independent woman and no one, neither Politics nor Commerce, told her what to do. Though she had a tendency to exaggerate, for once Media spoke no more than the truth: the truth being that most nights of the week Politics, Media and Commerce could be found in bed together.

As its status and influence increase, the media takes on many of the characteristics of traditional elites. Like the nobility of old, it is concentrated in a few hands and its responsibilities are small in proportion to its power. Awareness of its wealth and influence encourages a lordly insouciance, and the knowledge that it sets the tone in society puts a swagger in its step. It respects no superiors. Its stance towards properly constituted authority (Parliament) is as cavalier as its attitude towards the rights of individuals (questions of privacy) can be overbearing. And in common with traditional elites it is impatient of any restrictions on its activities, tending to see itself as above the law. Governments quail before the media as kings did before barons, for when barons join together in opposition the king is doomed.

Media grandees enjoy a free-wheeling style of life, which does not prevent them posing as the arbiters of morality. If they remain largely untouched by scandal it is mainly because, as used to be the case with politicians, no one would dream of publicizing any untoward behaviour. Again like the old nobility, the media sticks together, and discretion about the peccadilloes of individuals is as complete as the condemnation of the same failings in others is total and unhesitating. And like the airiest of aristocrats, media moguls have their whims and eccentricities: a hunch or personal prejudice can be enough to disgrace a celebrity, destroy a family or foreshorten a promising ministerial career. In common with many an ancestral figure, the media is convinced it speaks in the people's name, sometimes without going through the formality of ascertaining what the people think. The people will know what they think when the media tells them.

With the money, power and authority goes the glamour. The grubby, Bohemian image of journalism is largely gone. No longer is it a refuge for the second or third rate, a reluctant choice for graduates after politics, the judiciary and the higher civil service. Now the higher reaches of the media are a greasy pole to themselves, along which the talented and ambitious clamber. It is fashionable to mock the proliferation of 'media studies' in former polytechnics: more significant is the fact that the number of Oxford graduates going into the press or TV tripled from 1971 to 1994.

One can see the attractions. If power and income are computed together the rewards for the successful can be far greater than for politicians. Media careers can be precarious – an aspect of the whimsicality with which media grandees exercise their powers of patronage – but then volatility of employment and evanescent influence are characteristic of the new elites. Just as the latest art genius has his day at the Royal Academy, so a tabloid editor can have his day in the *Sun*, and there will never be any difficulty in replacing either when their day is done. And should the editor contrive to be successful over a long period, at the end of a career of playing to mass tastes, our anti-elite patricians can expect to be knighted or ennobled by a duly deferential government. Meanwhile the living is good. Media magnificos are driven about in limousines that make those of ministers of the crown seem modest by comparison. And when the moguls or their minions summon ministers to dine they accept eagerly, as grateful for a meal in a restaurant beyond their private means as they are for a kind word in the organ in question.

Even as they ask probing questions about jobs for the boys in politics, the media itself remains a bastion of patronage, and where ownership is concerned, an advocate of the hereditary principle. Now that the House of Lords is finally undergoing reform it is only in the press that power and influence are inherited along with money, and handed down from generation to generation. The fact that a large number of people are capable of writing a passable article or opinion piece, or of partaking in the production of this or that TV programme, makes the media a natural sphere of favouritism. Once a well-born gentleman would see to it, as a matter of course, that a relation was found a place in a prestigious regiment or exclusive club. Now such patronage is more likely to be exercised to give a foothold in the media to their daughters, nieces or cousins, in the form of a well-paid and not over-demanding post on a diary page of the press, or as a TV producer or researcher. Of political favouritism there is no need to speak.

In television the interaction between populist elites and the masses is at its most intimate and direct. The reason is that TV is by nature hyper-democratic. As one of the Goncourt brothers observed at the time of its invention, the point about photography was that 'anyone can look'. He was, of course, talking before the invention of the moving image, which magnified the attractions of photography a thousandfold, and almost a century before television placed the perpetually moving image in billions of homes. Still photographs entice the eye; TV mesmerizes it. Good programmes are normally described as 'compulsive viewing', yet it is not so much the programmes that are compulsive, it is the screen.

A balancing cliché has it that if the public do not like what they see there is nothing to prevent them ceasing to watch. Yet for the masses (which is to say the average viewer) there is no real option of switching off, in the way one would close a book or put down a newspaper and do something else. If they do not feel compelled to watch one programme the majority of viewers will watch another, and if it is not TV it is video. Yet another cliché speaks of 'a captive audience'. TV audiences are more than captive, they are subjugated: in thrall to the moving image, pretty much irrespective of what it depicts. And the non-selective element of television is not confined to the ease of looking: it is also there in the technical facility of filming and in the ease of filling the screen with whatever comes to hand. It is these three aspects of TV that make it a political/cultural tool of unrivalled power. Those who control it find themselves in the most enviable position it is possible to aspire to in a mass society: that of power elites in control of an anti-elite medium.

It was Martin Heidegger, of all people, who came up with the most suggestive definition of film and television. *Tele* meaning far off, his insight concerned the idea of distance. The point about TV, he wrote in his essay 'The Thing', was not that it brought far-off objects closer. Yet nor did it leave things where they were. TV banishes the concept of distance altogether, imposing, in Heidegger's words, a 'uniformity of non-distance in which everything will be carried away in confusion'. It is not difficult to think of day-to-day examples of what he meant. The shot of the woman who embodies your dreams does not bring her into your home. Yet the illusion that it does makes it impossible to think of her remaining where she was, in the TV studio, on the beach, in the intimacy of her bedroom. According to Heidegger, she ends up neither here nor there, suspended, as dreams are, in a 'uniformity of non-distance'.

The uniformity arises because, as the briefest flick through the channels shows, everything on TV is in permanent motion and yet everything appears the same. Seen this way, television becomes an egalitarian machine in a double sense. Accessible and popular ('anyone can look'), it also has a homogenizing effect, as hierarchies of meaning are abolished, as well as distance in a physical sense. In the turmoil of sense impressions, values are confounded. A zip through the programmes reveals a blur of meaningless colour, meaningless violence, politicians spouting meaningless phrases, singers crooning meaningless songs. TV is the defining influence of modern democracy and again there can be no better phrase to describe it than the one Tocqueville used to describe democracy itself: agitated and monotonous.

Somehow little of it seems to have anything to do with life. Reality has been yanked up by the roots and transported into some pale blue yonder where it floats and spins, like the satellites that beam the pictures down to us, in weightless, sterile space. The impression is one of extreme concreteness – who can argue with the 'truth' of an individual image? – and of permanent unreality. A simple instance conflates the two. What could be more factual and yet more unreal than the process of presenting the news? A good-looking person is selected to tell us what is happening in the world. If it is a woman she will be dressed in demurely sexy clothes, so as to appear like a cross between a dream wife, a mother and a mistress. If it is a man he will probably be less sexy, but will serve as a mature lover and father-figure too. Caked in make-up, they are seated behind a desk against a stage-like backdrop and coached like mynah birds to transmit to us from a teleprompter in uncannily exquisite tones the information that hundreds of refugees have been slaughtered, that Chelsea have beaten Arsenal and that the Bank of England has dropped interest rates by one quarter of one per cent.

It is a crazed procedure, a ludicrous sexing-up of reality, the kind of thing that Tristan Tzara or Ionesco would have guyed as surreal. In a newspaper readers would imbibe such information as they needed about football scores or interest rates in the blink of an eye; here they have a dream wife/mother/mistress or avuncular lover who is paid hundreds of thousands a year to win their hearts as he or she imparts the news. Still stranger things can be found on television, masquerading as high serious-ness. If you are bored by the news and would prefer a debate you may find yourself watching an edition of *Question Time*, chaired by the scion of a broadcasting dynasty, David Dimbleby, who holds the floor with statesmanlike dignity while a politician and a comedian dressed in drag talk about Iraq and its suffering children. As the drag artist intones the words *Saddam Hussein* or *medical treatment for the starving victims* the attention of many a viewer will be concentrated on his extravagantly arched eyebrows or saucy earrings. Again, an out-of-this-world spec-tacle, meriting the Tzara treatment.

If you were a conspiracy theorist of leftist inclinations, you might easily conclude that media elites, commercial interests and politicians were hand in glove to distract us from our rightful grievances against the system, by feeding us on fantasy. Yet that would be a fantasy in itself. Passivity and disengagement from the real may indeed be the result of such programmes, yet it by no means follows that this is the intention. The moguls do it because the average viewer prefers visual distraction to verbal reasoning. TV elites do it because they are anxious not to appear stuffy, i.e. elite. And television is the perfect vehicle for the entire fantastic concoction because, as Heidegger noticed, it lies in its nature to take reality by the scruff of the neck and cast it into the ether.

My argument is concerned mainly with television as a vehicle for populist exploitation, and I am far from condemning the medium out of hand (even if it were possible to condemn out of hand a box of tricks). Obviously there can be amusing, well-made or informative shows and documentaries. Given the tor-rential output and the two billion pounds the public is obliged to contribute through the licence fee it would be scandalous if there were not. Nor can one dismiss commercialism as a completely negative force. If the right amount of investment meets the right kind of talent in the most beneficent cultural circumstances superb programmes can result: a Murdoch company is responsible for *The Simpsons*. Yet as competition increases and quality declines, a glance at TV's most typical products might lead you to believe that large sections of the medium were staffed by mental defectives. This is far from being the case. The most popular form of entertainment devised by man is run by highly select people, most of them men and women of middle or upper-middle social origins with university degrees. The least one can say is that their education is not invariably reflected in what we see on the screen, and it is this that goes to the heart of the matter. TV is an ideal vehicle for condescension by anti-elite elites, and many of those who control it habitually play down to our emotions, down to our intelligence, down to our prurience, down to our credulity.

A few names make the point. The Chief Executive of Channel 5 TV is David Elstein. Elstein went to Aske's Haberdashers' School and graduated from Cambridge University with a first. Spoken of as a rising star in television, he was mentioned as a possible Director General of the BBC. This despite the fact that the channel he runs is noted for its soft porn films and low-grade entertainment – some of it so low grade that the Independent Television Commission last year took the unusual step of denouncing several of its programmes as 'tacky'. One of Elstein's productions, *Sex and Shopping*, was described as unsuitable for broadcasting at any time. (Whatever one thinks of its comic productions, the channel has one good crack to its credit. Asked about the suitability for broadcasting of a programme on the female orgasm, Dawn Airey, its programme director, who attended Kelly College and Cambridge, is said to have replied: 'The BBC does *The Human Body* as a science documentary. We do one specific part of it.')

Elstein dismissed the ITC complaint as 'anachronistic and patronising'. The exchange reveals the extent to which media oligarchs, like arts apparatchiks, live in an inverted world. Presumably Elstein meant that the Commission was patronizing the public by criticizing its tastes. Like the Chairman of the Arts Council, he appears to have forgotten that he himself is the patron, in the literal sense: the boss of a TV channel which was exploiting those tastes to attract the maximum number of viewers so that his channel would be judged a financial success, along with himself. (Needless to say, in this Elstein is succeeding.) So the patronizing is done by Elstein, who talks down to the masses, not by the ITC, who attempt to talk them up.

When he is not broadcasting populist entertainment, Elstein comes across as something of a patrician in a different sense, giving lectures on the media, expressing solidly conventional views on panel discussions or throwing off a reference to Wittgenstein in a newspaper article. When not titillating the masses with shows about the female orgasm, Airey voices high-minded convictions about broadcasting: 'My greatest fear is that the BBC will go the way public service broadcasting went in the States.' A dual persona – the educated, responsible citizen trumpeting social pieties, whose work involves the cultural impoverishment of the masses – is typical of new media elites. Their attitudes echo more primitive social times. Morally their position is not far removed from the nineteenth-century industrialists who urged their employees to chapel of a Sunday while paying them un-Christian wages.

Another example. Peter Bazalgette operates an independent TV company producing a range of programmes, some popular, some populist (the defining line, admittedly, can sometimes be a matter of taste). He went to Dulwich College and Cambridge, where he became President of the Union. Bazalgette is also seen as a promising talent in his industry, and is prominent in the campaign to lift quality restrictions on broadcasting imposed by the Independent Television Commission, which, like Elstein, he feels are too restrictive. There are signs that his aspirations may be somewhat higher than Elstein's, though we shall see. The tendency of well-educated folk to run mass-market media outlets is not limited to television. In parts of the tabloid press previously headed by journalists who had risen from the bottom a similar trend appears to be at work. It is a nice irony that the more gentrified a newspaper's management, the more vulgar it tends to become.

There is nothing much wrong with low-grade entertainment, prurient enquiries into our bodily functions or cheap sex shows, providing those who serve them up for (an excellent) living spare us their sermons about opening our minds or helping us discard our prudish inhibitions. Someone will always produce them, there will always be viewers, and such programmes satisfy a certain need. So it is not a matter of objecting to smut. Least of all is it specifically a question of where this or that media person went to school or university. What is new and significant is the energy with which fortunate, well-schooled folk set about 'making a career in the masses', and their lack of squeamishness when it comes to exploiting the tastes of people less well educated than themselves in the furtherance of those careers. Not long ago the holder of a Cambridge first or a President of the Union would have automatically gone into 'old elite' professions: politics, the higher civil service or the law. Elstein, Airey, Bazalgette and their ilk have made a canny choice. Ambitious men and women who have spotted the direction of events, they have clearly decided that their future lies with crowds.

It is revealing to compare attitudes to TV in Britain and abroad. In other countries television is often seen as an intrinsically playful medium: a Pandora's box of tricks from which absolutely anything may be made to spring. In the United States the box spews forth imbecilities of every kind. At the same time America produces some of the finest entertainment ever made, because the box of tricks is exploited to brilliant effect, and refuses to take itself over-seriously. In France TV has never prospered, or produced much of interest. Disdain for the small screen is shared by the intelligentsia of Left and Right, and until recently the top few per cent of society did not even own a set. With the exception of one or two series, such as the celebrated book programme *Apostrophes*, French TV had little to recommend it. It lacked both the British veneer of gravitas and the Americans' inspired frivolity. Now that its power is growing, and viewing figures have increased, its influence is contested from all quarters.

In his book *Television*, the philosopher Pierre Bourdieu mounted a ferocious attack on the medium, in the spirit of Marcuse's *One Dimensional Man*. He compared TV producers and journalists to Thersites, 'the ugly, cowardly thrower of words in the *Iliad*, who abuses everybody and argues nothing but scandal', and went on:

On the one hand TV lowers the 'entrance fee' in a certain number of fields – philosophical, juridical and so on . . . On the other hand, it has the capacity to reach the greatest number of individuals. What I find difficult to justify is the fact that the extension of the audiences is used to legitimate the lowering of standards for entry into the field. People may object to this as elitism, a simple defence of the besieged citadel of big science and high culture, or even as an attempt to close out ordinary people . . . In fact I am defending the conditions necessary for the production and diffusion of the highest human creations. To escape the twin traps of elitism and demagogy we must work to maintain, even to raise the requirements of the right of entry – the entry fee – into the fields of production.

The condemnation of TV's vulgarity by a man who would be seen here as a representative of the hard Left is suggestive. Again the difference with Britain comes down to varying concepts of egalitarianism. In the US television is understood to be an inherently populist medium and few pretend otherwise. In France intellectuals see TV as demeaning to the masses, who are thought to deserve better; for them it is a non-egalitarian medium since it does not allow simple people to raise their aspirations. In Britain, with our tendency to 'look down in satisfaction', the public are told (and tell themselves) that we have the best TV in the world. The answer to that is, yes and no. Being the best in the world is not saying much. It certainly does not mean that it is intellectually ambitious, and programmes that stretch the mind or imagination are increasingly few. Yet neither does it mean that we are on a level with the Americans' comic inventiveness. So it is that our most superior TV, pride of the race, imports the majority of its wittiest and most entertaining programmes from the USA. Which does not prevent us deriding American TV from a most superior height.

British TV is a genteel compromise. There is a curious priggishness in our television culture. A cloak of respectability is thrown over the small screen like a virginal dress on a lady of easy virtue, but the reality shows through. A few outstanding programmes excepted, much of the product is niminy-piminy stuff, neither low- nor high-brow, but somewhere towards the lower middle. The genius of British television is that it contrives to sound intelligent to the average man while consistently underrating the average man's intelligence.

The pretensions of TV elites form part of a wider culture of dissimulation. Television strains for respectability while serving up an undemanding diet in the way that writers of best-selling novels strain towards literary status. A feature of elites of all eras is their self-importance, and even as they titillate mass taste for profit or promotion our TV elites affect a weighty style. The tone in which TV mandarins discuss their plans to amuse or instruct the public is simultaneously pompous and vulgar. TV generates an aura of high seriousness to disguise the mediocrity of its intentions. As a result, this most banal and larky of mediums is invested with a dignity it neither needs nor deserves. The appointment of a new presenter (is he/she sexy enough?), the timing of news bulletins, the promotion or demotion of this or that broadcasting bureaucrat, the movement of a sports commentator from one channel to another – such TV trivia are discussed with the solemnity of matters of state, which indeed they have become. The same inflation is there in its most mundane techniques of production: to get a fifteen-second soundbite from a minor politician a small posse of producers, 'researchers' and technicians is involved.

Broadcasting eminences do not take kindly to having their pomposity pricked, and like elites of all eras are prone to quote the achievements of the past in justification of the *status quo*. The suggestion that public service broadcasting is not doing its job, and that quality is falling, provokes bristling indignation. Out come the counter-examples of Lord Clark's 'Civilization' series, *The Jewel in the Crown* or the overrated and voyeuristic creations of the late Dennis Potter. The truth is that these triumphs of the medium are both untypical of its daily fare and belong to an earlier, less populist era. Listening to TV notables quoting its proud history in support of its indifferent present reminds one of a hereditary peer seeking to justify his continued presence in the Lords by telling us that his great-great-grandfather had played a part in our victory at Waterloo.

Opening up TV to competition through digital broadcasting, independent producers and the rest may do something to democratize the means of ownership and production, and to challenge quasi-monopolies. What it seems most unlikely to do is to democratize the programmes themselves, in the best sense of the word: i.e. to show greater respect for the public's intelligence and potential. The competition seems all too likely to be downwards, and the variety strangely unvaried. One way and another it seems probable that we can look forward to more of the same, only more so. Meanwhile broadcasting elites will be numerically expanded, as new investors and producers scrabble for the commercial pickings. As frequently happens when upstarts threaten existing hierarchies, the newcomers will be denounced as vulgarians by the sleeker and glossier populists who have presided over matters till now. Their productions may indeed be of lesser quality, yet in a perverse sense one looks forward to the irruption of the TV barbarians. At least they will be less inclined to lace their language with sanctimony and more likely to admit that they are involved in a straightforward cash transaction with the masses. Vulgarity, on however low a level, is always preferable to cultural pretence.

Such is the pervasiveness of TV that radio and the print media increasingly strive to the condition of television: vivid imagery, colour, anecdotalism, immediacy, anti-intellectualism, an appeal to the senses rather than to the brain. For all its decline, however, the best parts of the press remain of a standard unmatched by television, and internationally impressive. There are few TV equivalents to the best of our reviewers, columnists, interviewers, war correspondents or leader or feature writers. Yet the downward pressures are growing, and there is an obvious analogy between the ratings war on TV and the circulation war in the press. Both are crowded markets where raw commercialism is increasingly in command, and editors and programmers have little hesitation in stooping low. One thing that can be said for the new elites in the media is that they are not afraid of getting their hands dirty.

The more powerful the press becomes, the more it must appear to speak with the people's voice. Hence a central ambivalence in its attitude towards authority. Even as they rival the government for influence, newspapers find themselves buttressing the dwindling power of politicians. The press needs politicians to assail as David needs Goliath, and even when David towers over the shrunken giant of government he must continue to assume the posture of a boy armed with a mere sling against Goliath's flailing club. This helps to explain the extraordinary coverage given to the sayings and doings of politicians, which though somewhat diminished is still excessive, whether it be gossip about sexual proclivities, prime ministerial babies or impending reshuffles. It also explains the tendency of the press to play up the powers of modern governments to do good or ill. In the same way that populists in culture and education are bound to exaggerate the strength of traditional elites to legitimize their demotic stances, so the media has a tendency to inflate the influence of the political Establishment to disguise the growth of its own. The overriding imperative is to keep the old up/down antinomies going, whereby the press are the defenders of the people and politicians their real or potential oppressors. The notion that a vulgarized press culture can itself be a form of oppression is not one that would be understood by media elites.

The fact that the press is in general more right-wing than radio or television does not, of course, mean that it is any less inclined towards populism. As the newspapers demonstrate on a daily basis, it is possible to run conservative and ultra-democratic horses in harness, which is scarcely to be wondered at, since ultra-democracy is in essence a reactionary creed. When it comes to selling newspapers, commercial imperatives eclipse ideology, and Conservative-supporting owners or editors are as happy to affect anti-elite postures as their left-wing brothers. In pursuit of power and profit the defenders of the old elites can find themselves behaving remarkably like the new. The results can be cant of an almost comical order. In right-wing broadsheets the editorial pages exhort the nation to preserve its hierarchical structures and traditions, and to maintain standards that are under attack from egalitarian forces in every sphere of our lives. Meanwhile much of the paper is given over to prurient articles or vacuous lifestyle features, to buoy up sales.

On the editorial pages, a valiant defence of the House of Lords, a column inveighing against sex education in schools or a High Tory view of the history and destiny of the Church of England. Several pages earlier we find ladies in lingerie, a particularly nasty rape case recounted in succulent detail or the confessions of a male prostitute. The message to readers is clear: providing they refrain from questioning inherited authority, attend church once in a while and pray God to smite our enemies, notably in Europe, the masses are allowed their diversions. Not only six days a week, but Sundays too.

8

Unsentimental Education

Democracy, by definition, cannot mean merely that an unskilled worker becomes skilled. It must mean that every citizen can govern, and that society places him, even if only abstractly, in a general position to achieve this.

Antonio Gramsci, *Prison Notebooks*

In Ionesco's play *Amédée ou Comment s'en Débarrasser?* (*Amédée or How to Get Rid of It?*) an anxious, elderly couple live in an apartment. The scene is fetid and enclosed – mushrooms grow on the ceiling – and gradually the reason for their anxiety becomes obvious. A corpse is concealed in an adjoining room. It is not clear whose it is: maybe they have committed a crime they are trying to forget, maybe it is a symbol of some terrible memory. The question is, how to get rid of it? It is no use pretending it is not there: to remind them, the corpse, colossally inflated, enters the scene gradually, feet-first, till it dominates the room and begins knocking over the furniture, and can no longer be ignored.

The corpse invading our memories, the old Left might say, is class; we pretend it is not there but it comes back to haunt us at every turn. In a sense the position is worse than that. A class system is in operation when people's lives are pre-determined by their social status. That is far less true than it was. As almost everyone will tell you, we have advanced well beyond those staid, constricting days, and are so much more equal than we were. Indeed it is hard to stop everyone telling you just how equal we have become. When people can't stop talking about a subject, something is on their minds.

The truth is that our society is permeated at every level, not so much by class, as by class inverted. So obsessed are we by equality (or its appearance) that it is hard to think of an era where class-consciousness was more acute. The thing itself may be dead or moribund but the thought of it won't let us alone, like poisoned memories. Each time we speak of the desirability of a classless society, or celebrate the fact that we have one, or argue about whether we have one or not, we are showing how relentlessly class haunts our minds. Each time we sniff the wind before speaking, to be sure we are in tune with mass opinion and will not risk sounding snobbish, we are displaying our neurosis. Whenever we give a downwards tweak to our public utterances (or to our public examinations), or surreptitiously adjust our dress or accent or taste in music to the norm, we are at it again. The people most likely to do it, it goes without saying, are those who are more equal than the rest. Guy Ritchie, Madonna's current boyfriend, is a nice example. It is not enough to be a good-looking, expensively educated person from a fortunate background, not enough to make a flying start to his film career with *Lock, Stock and Two Smoking Barrels*, not enough to have a global sex goddess for his girlfriend: to rub our noses in his all-round superiority, he affects a toffee-nosed proletarian accent.

A class-conscious society is a breeding ground for inverted elites. In radio or TV debates about class it is they who dominate the panels. Nine times out of ten the discussants are a pretty good class of person themselves, not because they are rich or toffs, but because they have enjoyed a sound education. Having attended private or selective schools they tend to be confident, articulate and cultivated above the norm. And, of course, they are immensely liberal-minded. That is why they are on the panel. There is a ritual quality to the discussions. Also a certain

wariness. The edginess is understandable, for the more determinedly the participants avert their faces, the more powerfully
one senses the corpse of class invading the room:

*Presenter: 'Let's start with you, Gillian. Would you agree
with this book that class is still an important factor in Britain
today?'*

*Gillian: 'I really don't know why we are discussing it. The
whole concept is dead. Look at the young! So much healthier
than our generation! My daughter wears the same clothes, likes
the same music and speaks the same English as everyone else . . .'*

*And so on she goes, for some time, in praise of the younger
generation. Gillian is a senior journalist and writer and a worthy
woman. Rebecca, her daughter, is a spoilt, selfish, indolently
clever adolescent. If Gillian speaks of Rebecca in tones of defiant
unconcern it is because she is not so much concerned as morti-
fied. It is true that the girl behaves exactly like everyone else,
and that is the problem. She is going through a phase that keeps
Gillian awake at nights and causes arguments with her husband.
Gillian takes Rebecca's side for the usual reasons: you have to
stick by them, otherwise . . . Like many liberal-minded professional parents she is deeply concerned with how her children
look, behave or articulate such thoughts as they may have – and
is damned if she is going to admit it. It wouldn't be so bad if
Rebecca were doing well at school, but she isn't. And when
Gillian hears her aping the latest street talk, or measures the
depth of vacancy in the eyes framed by her Walkman, she
experiences a twinge of angst. Can this really be their daughter?
The corpse of class is inching into her mind.*

Presenter: 'So you think the whole business is overdone.'

*Gillian: 'I can't think why we make such a fuss. Don't tell me
they don't have class systems in France and America. I've lived
there, I know.'*

*Careful now. Gillian is in danger of blustering. That is because
she doesn't really believe it is the same in other countries. She's*

lived there, she knows. Of course, they too can be class-conscious, but somehow, it's not the same.

Presenter: 'So your daughter prefers it here?'

Gillian: 'Rebecca – that's her name – couldn't wait to get back. Everyone's so much more relaxed here.'

The sound of the word makes Gillian feel more relaxed herself. She is doing well. Patriotism, faith in the young generation, can't go wrong. Will Rebecca be listening? Of course not, she never shows interest in anything her mother does, doesn't read a word she writes. Still, Gillian makes a mental vow not to say anything to suggest that she has values that are different from hers. She hasn't any values that are different, can't have values that are different, mustn't have different values, otherwise . . . [the shadow of the corpse]. Suddenly, she is uneasy again. If only the presenter would get away from this generation thing . . .

Presenter: 'Let's stick with this generation thing for a moment. Some parents – I don't mean you, Gillian – feel they have to go along with things they don't approve of. You know, so their children will feel comfortable in society.'

Oh for God's sake, Mr Presenter, you must have children yourself! You must know? What am I supposed to say? The truth? That it saddens my heart and martyrs my ear every time I hear her parrot some banal claptrap she's picked up in . . . [enter the corpse].

Gillian: 'I can't think of a single thing my daughter has done that has made me ashamed. I'm proud of her because she's fully integrated into society.'

By conforming to society's norms . . . Not something to be proud of, when you think of it, but on this subject Gillian has determined not to think.

Presenter: 'How far does education come into it?'

To the tune of £9,000 a year, Mr Presenter, if you want to know. And that's for day school. Maybe we should have sent her to boarding school. It would have cost even more and been a little embarrassing, but at least she would have been shut off

from . . . wouldn't have been able to waste all her time with . . .
[the corpse swells, begins knocking over the furniture].
   Gillian: *'Education? You mean private schools and all that?*
That's terribly overdone too.'
   Presenter: *'It says in this book –'*
   Gillian: *– 'I know what it says in the book. What I'm saying*
is that everyone has the same lifestyle today, no matter who
their parents are, or where they went to school, and I think it's
a very good thing.'
   Gillian sounds sincere. She has written thousands of words
on the theme, so she must believe it.
   Presenter: *'Thank you, Gillian . . .'*

Alas, poor Gillian, and her generation. Rebecca will be spared
this. Going to a private day school in central London has given
her the best of all worlds, made her a social hermaphrodite,
adapted to the times. Rebecca belongs simultaneously to a
higher and a lower sphere. In an ultra-democratic culture this
makes her doubly privileged. She is a product of that portion of
society that constitutes the *de facto* elite while appearing to
belong, when occasion demands, to the anti-elite majority. Her
parents have indulged her in every way, spending close to
£100,000 on her education. They themselves were meritocrats
in their time, but that does not confer sainted status: like aristocrats before them, meritocrats have a tendency to look after
their own, regardless of their merits. The £100,000 wasn't all
wasted. Rebecca has smartened up a bit, scraped into Oxford
(don't ask how), got a so-so degree.

   Her street-cred and parental contacts (and to a lesser extent
her degree) will ensure that she has no problem getting a job in
journalism, TV, the arts, the law, or as a commentator of some
description. If it is TV, she may help produce chat-shows or
pop extravaganzas. If she works in a theatre or art gallery,
she will help put on productions that critics will describe as
innovative/disturbing/challenging the foundations of society. If

it is the press, she will print or write reams of chat about royalty or girl power or rock. As social commentator she will inveigh against the kind of education she received. As a lawyer she will champion the (frequently educationally retarded) underdog. The truth is that Rebecca is only superficially bright, but never mind: her binary background gives her confidence beyond her merits, and she has more than lived down any stigma that attaches to her private schooling. So whatever she does she will soon be promoted. Over-promoted, perhaps. Meanwhile she will marry someone she met at university who is engaged in similar pursuits. With their joint income, plus a little help from mummy and daddy and other useful contacts, they will send their children to the best independent or selective schools they can squeeze them into. And the circle will begin again.

Such is the not-untypical progression of the scions of the new elites. The difference between mother and daughter is that, whereas for Gillian class was a corpse invading her conscience, for Rebecca it is definitively dead. This is progress of a sort. In her mother's era, guilt was a disease. To assuage it Gillian used to sit on the board of a comprehensive, which was good for her conscience, though less good for the school, since her egalitarian angst prevented her from helping it to raise its expectations. Rebecca will be too busy for all that. Nor will she need forcible contact with ordinary folk or popular culture. The masses are the sea in which she swims. Half a century ago the sons and daughters of the middle or upper-middle classes sometimes turned to socialism or communism by way of atonement. Today they make their career in the people, which is financially more rewarding and a lot more fun. The children of the new elites don't feel guilty any more. And so far as they do, the guilt has been turned to profit.

Educationally, Britain is a unique country. Nowhere else have 90 per cent of those in leading positions in society been educated in schools which 90 per cent of the current generation cannot attend. I have in mind not just the independent sector, which accounted for a mere 5 per cent in their day (7 per cent now), but highly selective grammars or direct grant schools. For all its social progress, educationally speaking Britain is still governed by an exclusive caste, not in the Old Etonian sense, but simply because the leaders of society in almost every field were educated in establishments set aside for them because they were talented and/or because their parents had money. Most of the Labour Cabinet went to grammar or independent schools. Virtually all the Shadow Cabinet except William Hague went to selective schools, mainly private. The same is true of our leading broadcasters, of almost every editor, of the most prominent people in the arts, of writers like Salman Rushdie and Martin Amis, the heads of our major firms, vice chancellors and the rest.

There is no need to get emotional about this. I state these things as matters of fact. Children do not choose where they are sent to school, and no stigma can attach to anyone lucky enough to have benefited from a sound education. Indeed it should be comforting to know that those who run our affairs are people who have enjoyed, by one means or another, the best schooling that was going. Yet things are not so simple. The elites we are discussing were segregated from their fellows (and in private boarding school, from society) from their early years, in a way for which there is no direct parallel in other countries. In France and Germany private schools are often denominational and not seen as educationally superior, and in Germany the technical schools, which produce doctors and engineers, are not comparable to our old secondary moderns, whose pupils tended to be treated as failures. No major country, in fact, suffers from the deep caesura we have between comprehensive and independent schools.

The problem for us is clear: how will our power elite, who have benefited from an education no longer open to the rest (unless they can afford private schools or a house in close proximity to one of the few remaining grammars) feel towards the less fortunate 90 per cent? If they are arrogant, they will not give it a thought because they see themselves as a superior caste. If they are enlightened, they may decide to use whatever influence they wield to open up horizons which have been closed for the many. Yet these two categories are likely to be exceptions. Most likely of all is that, consciously or otherwise, our educationally advantaged caste will compensate for their privilege by a plangent concern with equality for the common man. And if an excessive concern with equality in education has the perverse effect of perpetuating low standards, and thereby keeping the common man in his place, too bad for the common man.

All parents favour equal opportunity. It is just that, when it comes to their children, the principle ceases to apply. For parents to believe that other people's children are equal to their own would go against the laws of nature. What they want for them is *unequal* opportunity, and elites, new or old, are better placed than the average man and his wife to secure it. In higher education, the same unprincipled approach applies. The theory is that access should be equal to equal universities, yet no one who can afford it wants any such thing: they want privileged access to universities that are far from equal. The greater the distance between poor and excellent institutions, the more parents strive to secure places for their children in the good ones and to avoid the bad.

The British educational system could have been purpose-built for the emergence of the new elites, since it is one where egalitarian myth encourages a brute reality. The result of the abolition of grammar schools and of the myth that comprehensive schools are fine has been the flourishing of the private sector. The result of the myth that all institutions of higher learning are universities and that all universities are the same has been that an ivy league has grown vigorously, as ivy does. And the polarization between comprehensive and private sector education ensures that independent schools dominate the best universities to a greater degree than they did thirty years ago. In education, ultra-democracy goes along with social regression.

The culture of pretence invades every field of our lives, and in education the pretence is never-ending. The state sector pretends that the problem with comprehensives is primarily one of resources and that, given sufficient means, it could improve its performance to the point where private and selective schools would become redundant. This is what is known as an intellectual lie, which is to say something that otherwise honest folk have convinced themselves is true, even though they know perfectly well it is not, because it would be too painful to acknowledge the reality. In this case the reality is that there can be no radical improvement in state schools while the top of society is not involved. Private schools have their own version of the intellectual lie, namely the pretence that they are open to all (as if everyone could afford the fees), and that palliatives such as the Assisted Places Scheme overcame the social divisions. It goes without saying that the twin pretences are mutually sustaining.

Left-wingers complain about the snobbery of the private sector, but if that were the problem, it would be no problem. Not many people are ready to pay a small fortune to send their children to independent schools purely for the social cachet; £100,000 pre-tax income per secondary school child is a serious sum of money, even for a snob. The real 'problem' about the independent sector is its academic quality, relative to the state sector, not least because many girls' private schools have ceased being finishing schools and become serious places of learning. If (as the *Financial Times* estimated last year) all but thirteen of the top-performing 100 schools in the country in examination terms are in the private sector (and a good proportion of the thirteen were grammars), this is not simply because of 'better facilities' or smaller classes, though those are factors. It is because the ethos of independent schools is more aspirational.

Meanwhile a majority of children are locked into an intrinsically second-rate system of education, where everyone knows that the best examination results and a massively disproportion-ate number of places in the best universities will go year after year to the 7 per cent in private schools. It is scarcely surprising that class-consciousness remains rife, amongst the fortunate 7 per cent as well as amongst the educational underdogs, pupils as well as teachers. In state schools the resentment is reflected in anti-elite doctrines of education, which compound the prob-lem, as expectations decline relative to the elite sector. And since the laws of class inversion operate in the classroom as efficiently as elsewhere in society, the contagion spreads to private schools. In many an independent day school care is taken to include folksy fare on the English curriculum (a jokey Bill Bryson, a TV screenplay by Alan Bleasdale). Parents may wonder why they are paying for their children to study such easy meat, which they can get free at comprehensives, rather than pursuing a closer acquaintance with Keats or Eliot. Yet the schools know what they are about. Their task is to prepare what in many cases are destined to be the new elites for their careers in the masses, and it is desirable for them to be conversant with the culture of the people. In this way the most socially conscious private establishments can become 'finishing schools' in an inverted sense: this time the finishing involves not smoothing down, but roughening up.

In a strange way our two educational cultures are complemen-tary, as if the state and private sectors were working in accord-ance with a mutually agreed division of labour. By its levelling tendencies the state sector prepares the average pupil to limit his or her aspirations; by their more demanding curricula the private sector prepares society's new rulers, while prudently ensuring that they are not entirely divorced from the masses. It is easy to say that it was ever thus. But that, precisely, is the problem, and the division retains clear echoes of the situation of a hundred or more years ago.

The divide is much less wide than it was, and the overall standard higher, but in essence it is still there. How it is possible to have a truly democratic society with a two-tier education system in which the best schools are closed to the majority no one explains. When there is clearly no answer to a question, people give up asking. Which is what has happened to the discussion about the gap in achievement between state and private schools. *

Tacit collusion between Left and Right in favour of the *status quo* in our educational structures goes deeper. One of the over-simplicities of the British education debate is that the Left are against selection by merit, whereas it is a basic principle of the Right. Up to a point. It is true that all but the most advanced New Labourites remain against selection, narrowly defined. Yet despite policy statements to the contrary, the Right are half-hearted about anything approaching a truly meritocratic education system. It should never be forgotten that education is a supremely personal matter. Imagine for a moment a modernized system of selection by merit and aptitude, of the kind that exists in France or Germany, and that independent schools were included. Where would the children of Conservative MPs and party activists go to school, and which universities would they get into? If their meritocratic instincts had been as strong as they claimed the Tories would not have gone along with the destruction of the grammar and direct grant schools in the seventies as limply as they did, without attempting to put any-thing in their place, and would have used their eighteen years in power to re-impose selection in a more imaginative way than they did.

The truth is that no political party in Britain is in favour of a truly meritocratic system of education. Even when they them-selves were educated in grammar schools, the hearts of most

* In *We Should Know Better* (Fourth Estate, 1996), the author proposed a way of opening up private schools voluntarily to all the talents, regardless of their means. The Sutton Foundation, an educational charity established by the entrepreneur Peter Lampl, is running a pilot project at Belvedere School, an independent girls' school in Liverpool.

Tory MPs and of many of their ageing supporters are not in the state sector, any more than their children. Excess of zeal in re-inventing selective education, opening up private schools to all the talents or doing anything to challenge the dominance of private schools at top universities, would do little to help the prospects of their children. In practice, therefore, the Left and the Right are not unhappy with a two-tier system. The Left can nourish their resentments against the independent sector, and blame it for our national backwardness, and the Right can continue to benefit from a system which gives themselves and their children an easy pre-eminence, undisturbed by serious competition from below. The division may be deeply unsatisfactory for the country, but it is convenient for its political elites. All this is why the educational apartheid everyone dutifully laments is worse than it was thirty years ago, and why neither party has any serious plans to do anything about it. As international competition increases, the wastage of talent will cost us dear.

Half-truths and evasions about our two-tier system contaminate the discussion about elitism and elites. The consequences are predictable, notably in the cultural sphere. Here the highly literate graduate of Eton and Oxford writes columns deriding, in perfect sentences and impeccable cadences, the teaching of grammar. There an expensively educated cultural critic rhapsodizes about rap (modern plainsong), or the painterliness of Lowry (up there with Degas), or upbraids an author in rather closer touch with the masses than herself for failing to write about ordinary people in a sufficiently sympathetic manner. In addition to our cultures of pretence and of condescension, we have a culture of compensation too.

To 'educate' means to bring out, and there is nothing like education to bring out the hypocrisy of populist notables. Asked why he transported his children across half of London in order to send them to a grant-maintained, quasi-selective school, of the kind Labour insisted was divisive, Tony Blair's response deserves a place of distinction in the long annals of English cant: that he refused to impose political correctness on his children. To date that reply remains the most shameful thing he has said or done.

Ultra-democracies tend to speak in unctuous tones, and one of the most pervasive of their pieties is that parents are anxious for their children to receive a better schooling. This is one of those things it would be delightful to believe but for which evidence is lacking. The average parent is not especially anxious for their children to be well-educated, in the humanistic sense of the term. The reason for the upsurge of concern about standards is almost entirely economic – a natural reaction to technological competition and the job insecurity that goes with it.

In some countries (Russia, France) an idealist tradition of education for its own sake, though weakening, still endures. In Britain and America most people see schools and universities as places to get certificates and degrees necessary for employment. Armed with them their children have a better chance of success in worldly terms. They will buy the biggest house and car their incomes will stretch to, raise themselves in society and live as hedonistic a life as they can afford before they die. Why anyone should think such attitudes strange in a secular society dominated by market philosophies is strange itself.

Beneath an outward obeisance to tradition a vast and silent reassessment of the objectives of modern schooling is taking place. Except in regard to sex or citizenship, our hopes of moral, cultural or spiritual improvement through education are being quietly sloughed off. Kant saw education as the key to a free and enlightened society. Idealistic as this now seems, the dream was still there in the nineteenth century; the Workers' Educational Association did not confine itself to teaching humble folk to read or add up: it encouraged them to study Montesquieu, Helvetius, the literary classics. Today the WEA concentrates on picking up the pieces left by inadequate schooling and disastrous family backgrounds through remedial education; worthy though scarcely inspirational tasks.

Abdication of responsibility for raising the cultural levels of the average citizen is inherent in the actions and attitudes of the new elites. In education as in society (how could there be a difference?) the useful and the popular rule. When people speak of improving standards they mean first of all vocational studies; aspirations in the humanities remain at best stagnant. It is this that reconciles the calls by our ministers of education for ever higher levels of achievement with the deference of our ministers of culture towards mass taste. One aims up, the other down. The contradiction may seem glaring, though it makes a sort of lugubrious sense. How can we lament the shift from academic to vocational studies, which took another giant leap in the 1999 A-level examinations, when the rhetoric of government ministers and the media is aggressively utilitarian and anti-intellectual? What is the purpose of attempting to inculcate in the average child what postmodernists call the meta-narratives – grand stories about humanity and its culture – if the elites no longer believe in them?

It would be absurd to speak of a general lowering of standards: it is enough to watch the most unpromising child at play on a computer or fixing the video (it is amazing what the dimmest youngster can do when it wants to) to feel inferior. In the world of work, expectations are more demanding than they have ever been, and someone who would once have been a manual worker needs higher skills and qualifications today. Yet it should not be enough to treat children as clever technological monkeys. What matters is individual potential, in all spheres and at all social levels. It is increasingly assumed, and sometimes openly admitted, that it is a waste of time to seek to engage the majority in non-vocational studies. The implication is that most people will forever be helots of the economy and the entertainment industry, incapable of anything that may be remotely described as a higher life.

If this were a matter of choice it would matter less, but the helots are far from enjoying the same opportunities for self-advancement as their superiors. Such culture as they are deemed to need will be provided from above, by Mr Elstein and Ms Airey with their Cambridge degrees and their sex and shopping shows, or by the broadcasting speculators of the digital age. A glance around a typical council estate or modest street tells its tale. The houses of the helots hold forth their TV dishes like begging bowls to be filled by their social and educational betters, the new elites.

It is in education that hopes for the circulation of elites have been most obviously thwarted. The expectation was that, as free schooling spread, elites would include increasing numbers of meritocrats who had climbed a ladder whose summit was visible and whose rungs were recognized. When there are two cultures of education, and two ladders, the circulation becomes highly inefficient, or goes into reverse. People are still promoted on merit; it is just that the new meritocrats turn out with remarkable frequency to be the children of meritorious parents. The circulation of elites, it seems, has come to mean an elite that circulates very largely within itself. The upwardly mobile are dominated by those who are already close to the top, and the competition between them becomes a kind of run-off.

A single statistic makes the point. It is widely believed that the proportions of students at Oxbridge educated in private schools and state comprehensives is in the region of 50–50. That would be bad enough, given that 90 per cent of pupils attend comprehensives, but in fact the position is far worse. Only some 20 per cent of Oxbridge undergraduates are from state, non-selective schools. The rest come from fee-paying or quasi-selective schools and the few remaining grammars, themselves located by and large in prosperous areas. This situation has arisen because of a fundamental contradiction born of the sixties: the irreconcilability of egalitarianism in education and open elites. How can society be open to government by elites selected by merit when the practice and principles of state education, not to speak of the cultural tone of the times, is egalitarian, anti-selective, anti-elite (in the best sense of elite)? Again, one of those questions to which an answer has been unforthcoming for so long that we have given up asking.

Elites of whatever description tend to favour themselves, their families and their peers. It is inevitable that they should. They may also use their influence in myriad ways, many of them unconscious, to exclude others. In a truly democratic society that may seem hard to do, but that is not the society we live in, and the new elites have found a way. By their tolerance of low expectations in the state system of education, and their active encouragement of low expectations in culture or the media, they have pretty much excluded the majority from the competition. They do not do it deliberately, yet nor do they do it wholly by chance. They just do it. Whether they are leading opinion formers who denounce selection in state schools as elitist while their own children enjoy highly selective private education (remuneration for the robustly anti-elite article will pay the school fees for a month), or advocates of equality of access to the arts whose actions lead to a dilution of culture for the many, in effect they are covert apologists for the *status quo*.

A story to illustrate the point. As an education minister the author once gave a speech to an organization for the promotion of adult literacy. The audience, as always in such bodies, was dominated by charitably inclined members of the middle classes. He complimented them on their work, in all sincerity, but added that if all children were taught to read and write adequately at school their organization would have no need to exist. There are some statements of the obvious that it is inadvisable to make, and the audience did not take this one well. Faulty techniques of education, devised in the name of equality, were largely to blame for the proliferation of semi-literates, but such systemic failures they were disinclined to discuss or challenge. For many of those present what mattered was not so much literacy, it was their charitable posture, their top–down caring stance. They *needed* illiterates like a hospital needs patients, and were instinctively appalled at the thought of the supply drying up.

Beyond all the theorizing about elitism and elites lies a highly practical question. If it is admitted that elites are inevitable, and if those elites are drawn largely from a limited, introverted pool, how can we be sure that the nation is getting the best elite available? Obviously we cannot. Talent will remain unrecognized or, submerged by a sub-culture aided and abetted by the powers that be, go to waste. Meanwhile plausible mediocrities, such as our blithe Rebecca imagined above, will be given an easy ride to the top. On one point elitists and anti-elitists could surely make common cause: that nothing could be more detrimental to the interests of a society than to be run by elites unworthy of the name. Yet that, frequently, is what we have.

People have given thought to these things before, and their conclusions have not always been optimistic. In her essay 'The Crisis in Culture', Hannah Arendt wrote:

The relatively new trouble with mass society is perhaps even more serious, not because of the masses themselves, but because this society is essentially a consumer society where leisure time is used no longer for self-perfection or the acquisition of more social status, but for more and more consumption and for more and more entertainment. And since there are not enough consumer goods around to satisfy the growing appetites of a life process whose vital energy, no longer spent in the toil and trouble of a labouring body, must be used up by consumption, it is as though life itself reached out and helped itself to things which were never meant for it.

The result is of course not mass culture, which strictly speaking does not exist, but mass entertainment, feeding on the cultural objects of the world. To believe that such a society will become more cultured as time goes on, and education has done its work, is, I think, a fatal mistake. The point is that a consumers' society cannot possibly know how to take care of the world and the things which belong exclusively to the space of worldly experiences because its central attitude to all objects, the attitude of consumption, spells ruin to all it touches.

That was written in 1961, a time when the mass consumer society was in its infancy. If Arendt is right, and this society consumes culture in the destructive sense, the quality of the ruling elite ceases to matter. Whatever their personal ideals or preferences, they will end up by making a virtue of 'giving the people what they want'. In such a society genuine elites would be an embarrassment and an incongruity: a living rebuke to the masses, not to be tolerated.

The trouble with Arendt's argument is not that it is self-evidently wrong: it is that it paralyses action. She is more pessimistic than I would prefer to be. Is it really a 'fatal mistake' to believe that education can raise cultural norms, or that the advance of consumerism can some day be stalled? Surely much will depend on the lead – or lack of it – given by society's elites, notably in education. If we cannot invest any hope there, where else?

9

Late Thoughts

Elitism is democracy without the people. Populism is the people
without democracy.

Jacques Juillard, La Faute Aux Elites

Watching an old newsreel of Harold Macmillan or Alec
Douglas-Home broadcasting to the nation, it is difficult not to
smile. Were these leaders of a twentieth-century democracy? In
their presence even the microphones look anachronistic. They
might as well have been addressing a meeting of Victorian
charity commissioners. If the camera had swivelled on the public
to reveal men in top hats and women in bustles, they would
have seemed not so out of place. Yet it is a mere thirty-six years
since Macmillan was in power.

How will our new elites appear to us, thirty-six years hence?
Looking back on the old TV shots of the obsequious smiles,
hearing the honeyed voices exalting us, The People, for our large
souls and unparalleled creativity, will we laugh and think, as
we do with Macmillan or Douglas-Home: 'And they called *that*
a democracy? Who did they think they were kidding?' It would
be nice to believe it. I am conscious that my confidence in the
ability of society to resist the blandishments of the new elites
wavers at various points in this book. Our ruling oligarchy, far
larger than in the past, could be much harder to dislodge. Maybe
they are here for good? Perhaps we are entering a new phase of
history, in which the old laws of the circulation of elites no

longer hold. What if we get stuck with the kind we have, as technology gives them the means to perpetuate their power over a supine and indifferent public? What if flattery indeed gets you everywhere, and flattery of the people, for the people, by those posing as the people, becomes our natural mode of government?

Previous elites stirred emotions of envy, resentment, derision, but much of that is gone. How can you deride people who bathe you in a perpetual glow of approbation? How do you envy them for their riches when they are mostly not as rich as elites in the past? And how can you resent them for insisting on giving you what you want? The problem with populism, to repeat the point made in the preface, is that it tends to be popular. There is a disillusionment with politics, yet politics are not life, and in their material existence, for the moment most people have little reason to be despondent. They are more secure and longer-living than ever before. The large majority are eating well, in work, shopping, travelling, being entertained, distracting themselves. Most have more than sufficient unto the day, and choose the entertainments they do because they enjoy them. If they are victims of populism they do not appear to be suffering overmuch. On the contrary, they seem contented. What could be more arrogant than to worry about the nature of other people's contentment, or to suspect it of secreting a high bovine complement? And what could be more futile and fatuous than to set out to make contented folk discontented?

Never has it been more tempting or rewarding to shut up, relax and go with a tide that few seem anxious to resist and that there seems not the remotest prospect of redirecting. Private misgivings (if any) are easily concealed beneath the mask appropriate to the times: a set, ironic rictus. The difficulty is that the rictus can be wearying, and the irony can come to mask a feeling of estrangement from the mass-minded men and women a *laissez-faire* populism can help create. What began as a tolerant, liberal stance towards society and its prevailing culture can turn out to be something very different. Look closer and you will discover, more often than not, that cynicism is being passed off as tolerance and that the liberality disguises a neo-patrician insouciance. A flamboyant open-mindedness can be an excellent means of liberating ourselves from problems we feel are not our own and which we would prefer not to think about, and a modishly postmodern detachment can turn out to be more vertical than horizontal. In other words, elitism in disguise. 'If it amuses them, let them get on with it.'

All this is based on the supposition that a top–down populism is so ingrained in our culture as to be irremovable, and that technology will make it worse. On the more reasonable assumption that nothing lasts for ever, and that cultures change, hope becomes possible. For if our iron law holds true – the law that elites are inevitably replaced by history, that graveyard of aristocracies – at some point the reign of our populist monarchs will be over, or their power will decline. The fact that they feed on fashion could hasten their demise, and as with fashion, there doesn't even have to be a logical reason for change.

Maybe our egalitarian elites will prove a generational phenomenon, whose hypocrisies and insincerities will be exploded early in this century, much as those of Victorian patriarchs were at the turn of the last. Here and there are signs of fatigue, not least amongst the young, and parents who condescend to their childrens' tastes (inverted elites in their domestic setting) are finding things harder going. At the same moment a cultural restlessness, not confined to the frumpish or fractious middle-aged, is growing. What direction it will take is unsure, though whether the dissatisfaction relates to the quality of newspapers or television, popular music or the English novel, the tone of the complaint appears increasingly the same: 'Surely we can do better than this?'

And our power elites do not march in a phalanx. Like others before it, the new Establishment has its dissenting spirits. Far from volunteering to play down to the masses, such people find themselves press-ganged into the role. There is no more desolating position than to find oneself trapped between the crowd-pleasers and the crowd, and we should spare a thought for those who serve the new elites *à contre cœur*. Increasingly they are to be found at intermediate levels of their professions, which is sad but natural, since in culture and the media, as in politics, it is the conformists who get on.

The new counter-culture includes publishers who do their best to publish books on account of their worth rather than their likely sales, and for the moment still succeed; critics who say precisely what they think about the latest must-read novel or, even braver, decline to read it; dons with no smarmily populist agenda; juries who give prizes to difficult as opposed to infantilizing works; radio or TV personnel who persist in their ambitions to produce worthwhile programmes, and who get them broadcast; and journalists who, just once in a while, manage to knock royalty, sex and scandal off the front pages. There is even a handful of politicians who persistently decline the populist whip. Many of these folk can be recognized by a kind of pugnacious fatalism that afflicts all recalcitrants who work from within the system.

Then there is our sense of the absurd. How long will it be before the fawners on the people are seen as figures of fun? There must be a limit to the amount of patronizing a free people can take from its leaders, assuming it wants to be truly free. Finally there are the effects of time. Our leading demagogues, children of the sixties, will soon be long in the tooth, and already there are crow's-feet at the corners of those perpetual smiles. Surely the next generation of elites will find something better to do than to play out their parents' anti-elite charades? The tedium would be unendurable. For in the end what changes public cultures is the boredom factor. Cyril Connolly said that the British are patient folk, but when they decide they have had enough of something they give a great sigh and that thing is done with for ever. The time for a huge, collective sigh cannot come soon enough.

Sadly, the recent debate about Laura Spence and university entrance will bring sustenance to the anti-elites. There is certainly a problem about the narrowness of Oxbridge recruitment, though if anti-elitism is a euphemism for resentment of excellence, everyone will lose. As always, Right and Left were equally wary about going to the source of the problem: the state–private divide in schools and how it might be overcome. In weeks of furious commentary the great British taboo was never mentioned. Watching the country enjoying a reprise of class conflict, like some raucous minuet, no one would have guessed that it is populism, not elitism, that is at the heart of its problems.

Whether genuine or ultra-democracy prevails will not be decided simply by politics or economics, but by culture in the widest possible sense. I know of no adequate definition of the word, but for the purposes of this book the best I have seen comes from a report issued some years ago by the Collège de France:

One of the main functions of culture is that of a means of defence against all forms of pressure – ideological, political or religious. It is an instrument of free thought which, like the martial arts in other fields, can help today's citizen protect himself against the symbolic abuses of power to which he is subjected – advertising, propaganda and political or religious fanaticism.

In an age when the abuse of power endured by the common man comes from his loudest champions, he will need all the means of defence he can get.